AMERICAN POLITICAL, ECONOMIC, AND SECURITY ISSUES

SUPREME COURT APPOINTMENT PROCESS (UPDATE)

American Political, Economic, and Security Issues

Additional books in this series can be found on Nova's website at:

https://www.novapublishers.com/catalog/index.php?cPath=23_29&seriesp=American+Political%2C+Economic%2C+and+Security+Issues

Additional E-books in this series can be found on Nova's website at:

https://www.novapublishers.com/catalog/index.php?cPath=23_29&seriespe=American+Political%2C+Economic%2C+and+Security+Issues

AMERICAN POLITICAL, ECONOMIC, AND SECURITY ISSUES

SUPREME COURT APPOINTMENT PROCESS (UPDATE)

EMILIA S. DURAND
EDITOR

Nova Science Publishers, Inc.
New York

LIBRARY OF CONGRESS CATALOGING-IN-PUBLICATION DATA

Supreme Court appointment process (update) / editor, Emilia S. Durand.
p. cm.
Includes index.
ISBN 978-1-60876-934-6 (softcover)
1. United States. Supreme Court--Officials and employees--Selection and appointment. 2. Judges--Selection and appointment--United States. 3. United States. Supreme Court--Officials and employees--History. I. Durand, Emilia S. II. Rutkus, Denis Steven. Supreme Court appointment process. III. Smelcer, Susan Navarro. Supreme Court justices.
KF8742.S9118 2010
347.73'2634--dc22

2010012298

Published by Nova Science Publishers, Inc. ✦ New York

CONTENTS

PREFACE

The appointment of a Supreme Court Justice is an event of major significance in American politics. Each appointment is important because of the enormous judicial power the Supreme Court exercises as the highest appellate court in the federal judiciary. Appointments are usually infrequent, as a vacancy on the nine-member Court may occur only once or twice, or never at all, during a particular President's years in office. Under the Constitution, Justices on the Supreme Court received lifetime appointments. This new book reviews the procedure for the appointing a Supreme Court Justice.

Chapter 1 - The appointment of a Supreme Court Justice is an event of major significance in American politics. Each appointment is important because of the enormous judicial power the Supreme Court exercises as the highest appellate court in the federal judiciary. Appointments are usually infrequent, as a vacancy on the nine-member Court may occur only once or twice, or never at all, during a particular President's years in office. Under the Constitution, Justices on the Supreme Court receive lifetime appointments. Such job security in the government has been conferred solely on judges and, by constitutional design, helps insure the Court's independence from the President and Congress.

The procedure for appointing a Justice is provided for by the Constitution in only a few words. The "Appointments Clause" (Article II, Section 2, clause 2) states that the President "shall nominate, and by and with the Advice and Consent of the Senate, shall appoint ... Judges of the supreme Court." The process of appointing Justices has undergone changes over two centuries, but its most basic feature—the sharing of power between the President and Senate—has remained unchanged: To receive lifetime appointment to the Court, a candidate must first be nominated by the President and then confirmed by the Senate. Although not mentioned in the Constitution, an important role is played midway in the process (after the President selects, but before the Senate considers) by the Senate Judiciary Committee.

On rare occasions, Presidents also have made Court appointments without the Senate's consent, when the Senate was in recess. Such "recess appointments," however, were temporary, with their terms expiring at the end of the Senate's next session. The last recess appointments to the Court, made in the 1950s, were controversial because they bypassed the Senate and its "advice and consent" role.

The appointment of a Justice might or might not proceed smoothly. From the first appointments in 1789, the Senate has confirmed 122 out of 158 Court nominations. Of the 36 unsuccessful nominations, 11 were rejected in Senate roll-call votes, while nearly all of the rest, in the face of committee or Senate opposition to the nominee or the President, were withdrawn by the President or were postponed, tabled, or never voted on by the Senate.

Over more than two centuries, a recurring theme in the Supreme Court appointment process has been the assumed need for excellence in a nominee. However, politics also has played an important role in Supreme Court appointments. The political nature of the appointment process becomes especially apparent when a President submits a nominee with controversial views, there are sharp partisan or ideological differences between the President and the Senate, or the outcome of important constitutional issues before the Court is seen to be at stake.

Chapter 2 - On May 1, 2009, Justice David H. Souter announced his retirement as an Associate Justice when the U.S. Supreme Court recessed for the summer. To fill this vacancy, President Barack Obama selected Sonia Sotomayor, a judge from the U.S. Court of Appeals for the Second Circuit. In announcing the nomination, President Obama noted her Ivy League education and extensive judicial experience. President Obama also emphasized Sotomayor 's life story, discussing in particular her upbringing as a child of Puerto Rican-born parents in a Bronx housing project.

The Sotomayor nomination raised the prospect that, with her appointment, the nine-member Court would again have two female Justices and the first Justice to identify as Latina. The Sotomayor nomination also prompted renewed discussion among Senators, media commentators, and scholars regarding racial, ethnic, gender, religious, professional, and educational diversity on the Court. Against the backdrop of the Sotomayor nomination, this report examines the social, professional, and educational backgrounds of the Justices across the entire history of the Supreme Court.

Over time, the Supreme Court has become more diverse in some ways and more homogeneous in others. When first constituted, and throughout most of its history, no women or minorities served on the Court. This changed with the appointment of the first African-American Justice, Thurgood Marshall, in 1967, and the first female Justice, Sandra Day O'Connor, in 1981. When Justice Marshall retired from the Court in 1991, he was succeeded by another African-American, Justice Clarence Thomas. Although Justice O'Connor, upon her retirement in 2006, was succeeded by a male, Justice Samuel A. Alito Jr., the Court's membership once again, in August 2009, included two female Justices, upon the confirmation of Sonia Sotomayor.

In: Supreme Court Appointment Process (Update) ISBN: 978-1-60876-934-6
Editors: Emilia S. Durand

Chapter 1

SUPREME COURT APPOINTMENT PROCESS: ROLES OF THE PRESIDENT, JUDICIARY COMMITTEE, AND SENATE*

Denis Steven Rutkus

SUMMARY

The appointment of a Supreme Court Justice is an event of major significance in American politics. Each appointment is important because of the enormous judicial power the Supreme Court exercises as the highest appellate court in the federal judiciary. Appointments are usually infrequent, as a vacancy on the nine-member Court may occur only once or twice, or never at all, during a particular President's years in office. Under the Constitution, Justices on the Supreme Court receive lifetime appointments. Such job security in the government has been conferred solely on judges and, by constitutional design, helps insure the Court's independence from the President and Congress.

The procedure for appointing a Justice is provided for by the Constitution in only a few words. The "Appointments Clause" (Article II, Section 2, clause 2) states that the President "shall nominate, and by and with the Advice and

* This is an edited, reformatted and augmented version of a CRS Report for Congress publication dated May 2009.

Consent of the Senate, shall appoint ... Judges of the supreme Court." The process of appointing Justices has undergone changes over two centuries, but its most basic feature—the sharing of power between the President and Senate—has remained unchanged: To receive lifetime appointment to the Court, a candidate must first be nominated by the President and then confirmed by the Senate. Although not mentioned in the Constitution, an important role is played midway in the process (after the President selects, but before the Senate considers) by the Senate Judiciary Committee.

On rare occasions, Presidents also have made Court appointments without the Senate's consent, when the Senate was in recess. Such "recess appointments," however, were temporary, with their terms expiring at the end of the Senate's next session. The last recess appointments to the Court, made in the 1950s, were controversial because they bypassed the Senate and its "advice and consent" role.

The appointment of a Justice might or might not proceed smoothly. From the first appointments in 1789, the Senate has confirmed 122 out of 158 Court nominations. Of the 36 unsuccessful nominations, 11 were rejected in Senate roll-call votes, while nearly all of the rest, in the face of committee or Senate opposition to the nominee or the President, were withdrawn by the President or were postponed, tabled, or never voted on by the Senate.

Over more than two centuries, a recurring theme in the Supreme Court appointment process has been the assumed need for excellence in a nominee. However, politics also has played an important role in Supreme Court appointments. The political nature of the appointment process becomes especially apparent when a President submits a nominee with controversial views, there are sharp partisan or ideological differences between the President and the Senate, or the outcome of important constitutional issues before the Court is seen to be at stake.

BACKGROUND

The appointment of a Supreme Court Justice is an event of major significance in American politics. Each appointment to the nine-member Court is significant because of the enormous judicial power that the Court exercises, separate from, and independent of, the executive and legislative branches. While "on average, a new Justice joins the Court almost every two years,"[1] the time at which any given appointment will be made to the Court is unpredictable. Appointments may be infrequent (with a vacancy on the Court occurring only once or twice, or even never at all, during a particular President's years in office)[2] or occur in close proximity to each other (with a particular President afforded several opportunities to name persons to the Court).[3]

Early in his presidency, Barack Obama was afforded an opportunity to make his first appointment to the Court. On May 1, 2009, the 101st day of the Obama Administration, Associate Justice David H. Souter notified the President of his intention to retire from the Court when it concludes its current term.[4] Upon receiving this news, President Obama, at a press briefing, declared that "the process of selecting someone to replace Justice Souter is among my most serious responsibilities." In making this decision, he intended to "consult with members of both parties across the political spectrum." Also, the President said, it was his hope "that we can swear in our new Supreme Court justice in time for him or her to be seated by the first Monday in October when the Court's new term begins."[5]

Under the Constitution, Justices on the Supreme Court hold office "during good Behaviour,"[6] in effect receiving lifetime appointments. Once confirmed, Justices may hold office for as long as they live or until they voluntarily step down. Such job security in the federal government is conferred solely on judges and, by constitutional design, is intended to insure the independence of the federal judiciary, including the Supreme Court, from the President and Congress.[7] A President has no power to remove a Justice or judge from office. A Supreme Court Justice may be removed by Congress, but only through the process of impeachment by the House and conviction by the Senate. Only one Justice has ever been impeached (in an episode which occurred in 1804), and he remained in office after being acquitted by the Senate.[8] Many Justices serve for 20 to 30 years and sometimes are still on the Court decades after the President who nominated them has left office.[9]

The procedure for appointing a Justice to the Supreme Court is provided for in the Constitution of the United States in only a few words. The "Appointments Clause" in the Constitution (Article II, Section 2, Clause 2) states that the President "shall nominate, and by and with the Advice and Consent of the Senate, shall appoint ... Judges of the supreme Court."[10] While the process of appointing Justices has undergone some changes over two centuries, its most essential feature— the sharing of power between the President and the Senate—has remained unchanged: To receive lifetime appointment to the Court, one must first be formally selected ("nominated") by the President and then approved ("confirmed") by the Senate. Although not mentioned in the Constitution, an important role is also played midway in the process—after the President selects, but before the Senate as a whole considers the nominee—by the Senate Judiciary Committee. Since the end of the Civil War, almost every Supreme Court nomination received by the Senate has first been referred to and considered by the Judiciary Committee before being acted on by the Senate as a whole.

For the President, the appointment of a Supreme Court Justice can be a notable measure by which history will judge his Presidency.[11] For the Senate, a decision to confirm is a solemn matter as well, for it is the Senate alone, through its "Advice and Consent" function, without any formal involvement of the House of Representatives, which acts as a safeguard on the President's judgment. Traditionally, the Senate has tended to be less deferential to the President in his choice of Supreme Court Justices than in his appointment of persons to high executive branch positions.[12] The more exacting standard usually applied to Supreme Court nominations reflects the special importance of the Court, coequal to and independent of the presidency and Congress. Senators are also mindful that, as noted earlier, Justices—unlike persons elected to legislative office or confirmed to executive branch positions—receive lifetime appointments.[13]

Table 1. Current Members of the Supreme Court of the United States

Name	State[a]	Date of birth	Appointing President	Date Senate confirmed	Vote to confirm
John G. Roberts Jr. (Chief Justice)	MD	Jan. 27, 1955	Bush, George W.	Sep. 29, 2005	78-22
John Paul Stevens	IL	Apr. 20, 1920	Ford	Dec. 17, 1975	98-0
Antonin Scalia	VA	Mar. 11, 1936	Reagan	Sep. 17, 1986	98-0
Anthony M. Kennedy	CA	July 23, 1936	Reagan	Feb. 3, 1988	97-0
David H. Souter	NH	Sep. 17, 1939	Bush, George H.W.	Oct. 2, 1990	90-9
Clarence Thomas	VA	June 23, 1948	Bush, George H.W.	Oct. 15, 1991	52-48
Ruth Bader Ginsburg	DC	Mar. 15, 1933	Clinton	Aug. 3, 1993	96-3
Stephen G. Breyer	MA	Aug. 15, 1938	Clinton	July 29, 1994	87-9
Samuel A. Alito Jr.	NJ	Apr. 1,	Bush, George W.	Jan. 31, 2006	58-42

a. State of Justice's residence at time of appointment.

The appointment of a Supreme Court Justice might or might not proceed smoothly. Since the appointment of the first Justices in 1789, the Senate has confirmed 122 Supreme Court nominations out of 158 received.[14] Of the 36 nominations which were not confirmed, 11 were rejected outright in roll-call votes by the Senate, while nearly all of the rest, in the face of substantial committee or Senate opposition to the nominee or the President, were withdrawn by the President, or were postponed, tabled, or never voted on by the Senate.[15] Six of the unconfirmed nominations, however, involved individuals who subsequently were re-nominated and confirmed.[16]

From the presidency of George Washington until early in the 20th century, the Senate took final action on the vast majority of Supreme Court nominations within one week of receiving them. In recent decades, by contrast, the Senate has tended to proceed much more slowly. From 1967 through 2006 (the year of the most recent Supreme Court confirmation), 13 of the 21 Court nominations that advanced to the committee hearing stage were pending in the Senate for more than nine weeks before receiving final action.[17] The contemporary Senate's inclination to proceed more slowly with Supreme Court nominations has been due at least in part to several developments:

- Starting with the "Warren Court" in the 1950s (under then-Chief Justice Earl Warren), the Supreme Court became an ongoing focal point of controversy, as it handed down a succession of rulings ushering in profound changes in American society and politics. By the late 1960s, the perceived potency of the Court as a catalyst for change underscored to many Senators, especially those on the Judiciary Committee, the importance of closely evaluating the attitudes and values of persons nominated to serve on the Court.[18]
- A general trend among Senate committees, beginning in the 1970s and 1980s, was to intensify their scrutiny of presidential nominations and to augment their investigative staffs for this purpose. Thorough and unhurried examination was regarded as especially justified in the case of Supreme Court nominations. Accordingly, close scrutiny by the Senate Judiciary Committee became the norm, even if a nominee were highly distinguished and untouched by controversy.
- Many, if not most, of the nominees in recent decades proved to be controversial because of questions raised concerning their backgrounds, qualifications, or ideological orientation.
- It has become increasingly common for Presidents to state the philosophical or ideological values that they look for in a Supreme

Court nominee—a practice which may immediately raise concerns about the nominee on the part of Senators who do not share the President's philosophical preferences or vision for the Court.

- Many Court appointments in recent decades were made during times of "divided government," when one political party controlled the White House and the other was in the majority in the Senate.
- The frequency of 5-4 decisions by the Court has underscored to Senators how important even just one new appointment might be for future Court rulings.

PRESIDENT'S SELECTION OF A NOMINEE

The need for a Supreme Court nominee arises when a vacancy occurs on the Court, due to the death, retirement, or resignation of a Justice (or when a Justice announces the intention to retire or resign).[19] It then becomes the President's constitutional responsibility to select a successor to the vacating Justice.[20]

The Role of Senate Advice

Constitutional scholars have differed as to how much importance the Framers of the Constitution attached to the word "advice" in the phrase "advice and consent." The Framers, some have maintained, contemplated the Senate performing an advisory, or recommending, role to the President prior to his selection of a nominee, in addition to a confirming role afterwards.[21] Others, by contrast, have insisted that the Senate's "advice and consent" role was meant to be strictly that of determining, after the President's selection had been made, whether to approve the President's choice.[22] Bridging these opposing schools of thought, another scholar recently asserted that the "more sensible reading of the term 'advice' is that it means that the Senate is constitutionally entitled to give advice to a president on whom as well as what kinds of persons he should nominate to certain posts, but this advice is not binding."[23] Historically, the degree to which Senate advice has been sought or used has varied, depending on the President.

It is a common, though not universal, practice for Presidents, as a matter of courtesy, to consult with Senate party leaders as well as with members of the Senate Judiciary Committee before choosing a nominee.[24] Senators who candidly inform a President of their objections to a prospective nominee may help in identifying shortcomings in that candidate or the possibility of a confirmation battle in the Senate, which the President might want to avoid. Conversely, input from the Senate might draw new Supreme Court candidates to the President's attention, or provide additional reasons to nominate a person who already is on the President's list of prospective nominees.[25]

As a rule, Presidents are also careful to consult with a candidate's home-state Senators, especially if they are of the same political party as the President. The need for such care is due to the longstanding custom of "senatorial courtesy," whereby Senators, in the interests of collegiality, are inclined, though not bound, to support a Senate colleague who opposes a presidential nominee from that Member's state. While usually invoked by home-state Senators to block lower federal court nominees whom they find unacceptable, the custom of "senatorial courtesy" has sometimes also played a part in the defeat of Supreme Court nominations.[26]

Besides giving private advice to the President, Senators may also counsel a President publicly. A Senator, for example, may use a Senate floor statement or issue a statement to the news media indicating support for, or opposition to, a potential Court nominee, or type or quality of nominee, for the purpose of attracting the President's attention and influencing the President's choice.[27]

Advice from Other Sources

Advice, it should be noted, may come to Presidents not only from the Senate but from many other sources. One key source of influence may be high-level advisers within the President's Administration.[28] Others who may provide advice include House Members, party leaders, interest groups, news media commentators, and, periodically, Justices already on the Court.[29] Presidents are free to consult with, and receive advice from, whomever they choose.

Criteria for Selecting a Nominee

While the precise criteria used in selecting a Supreme Court nominee vary from President to President, two general motivations appear to underlie the choices of almost every President. One is the desire to have the nomination serve the President's political interests (in the partisan and electoral senses of the word "political," as well as in the public policy sense); the second is to demonstrate that a search was successfully made for a nominee having the highest professional qualifications.

Virtually every President is presumed to take into account a wide range of political considerations when faced with the responsibility of filling a Supreme Court vacancy. For instance, most Presidents, it is assumed, will be inclined to select a nominee whose political or ideological views appear compatible with their own. "Presidents are, for the most part, results-oriented. This means that they want Justices on the Court who will vote to decide cases consistent with the president's policy preferences."[30] The President also may consider whether a prospective nomination will be pleasing to the constituencies upon whom he especially relies for political support or whose support he would like to attract. For political or other reasons, such nominee attributes as party affiliation, geographic origin, ethnicity, religion, and gender may also be of particular importance to the President.[31] A President also might take into account whether the existing "balance" among the Court's members (in a political party, ideological, demographic, or other sense) should be altered. The prospects for a potential nominee receiving Senate confirmation are another consideration. Even if a controversial nominee is believed to be confirmable, an assessment must be made as to whether the benefits of confirmation will be worth the costs of the political battle to be waged.[32]

Most Presidents also want their Supreme Court nominees to have unquestionably outstanding legal qualifications. Presidents look for a high degree of merit in their nominees not only in recognition of the demanding nature of the work that awaits someone appointed to the Court,[33] but also because of the public's expectations that a Supreme Court nominee be highly qualified.[34] With such expectations of excellence, Presidents often present their nominees as the best person, or among the best persons, available.[35] Many nominees, as a result, have distinguished themselves in the law (as lower court judges, legal scholars, or private practitioners) or have served as Members of Congress, as federal administrators, or as governors.[36] Although neither the Constitution nor federal law requires that a Supreme Court Justice be a lawyer, every person nominated to the Court thus far has been.[37] A President's search for excellence in a nominee, however, rarely proceeds without also taking political factors into account. Rather, "more typically," a President "seeks the best person from among a list of those who fulfill certain of these other [political] criteria and, of course, who share a president's vision of the nation and the Court."[38]

Closely related to the expectation that a Supreme Court nominee have excellent professional qualifications are the ideals of integrity and impartiality in a nominee. Most Presidents presumably will be aware of the historical expectation, dating back to Alexander Hamilton's pronouncements in the *Federalist Papers*, that a Justice be a person of integrity who is able to approach cases and controversies impartially, without personal prejudice.[39] In that same spirit, a bipartisan study commission on judicial selection in 1996 declared that it was "most important" to appoint judges who were not only learned in the law and conscientious in their work ethic but who also possessed "what lawyers describe as 'judicial temperament.'" This term, the commission explained, "essentially has to do with a personality that is evenhanded, unbiased, impartial, courteous yet firm, and dedicated to a process, not a result."[40] Accordingly, Presidents sometimes will cite the integrity or fairness of Supreme Court nominees to buttress the case for their appointment.[41]

A President, as well, may have additional concerns when the Supreme Court vacancy to be filled is that of the Chief Justice. Besides requiring that a candidate be politically acceptable, have excellent legal qualifications, and enjoy a reputation for integrity, a President might be concerned that his nominee have proven leadership qualities necessary to effectively perform the tasks specific to the position of Chief Justice. Such qualities, in the President's view, could include administrative and human relations skills, with the latter especially important in fostering collegiality among the Court's members. The President also might look for distinction or eminence in a Chief Justice nominee sufficient to command the respect of the Court's other Justices, as well as to further public respect for the Court. A President, too, might be concerned with the age of the Chief Justice nominee, requiring, for instance, that the nominee be at least of a certain age (to insure an adequate degree of maturity and experience relative to the other Justices) but not above a certain age (to allow for the likely ability to serve as a leader on the Court for a substantial number of years).[42]

Background Investigations

An important part of the selection process involves investigating the background of prospective nominees. In recent years the investigative effort generally has followed two primary tracks—one concerned with the public record and professional credentials of a person under consideration, the other with the candidate's private background. The private background investigation, which includes examination of a candidate's personal financial affairs, is conducted by the Federal Bureau of Investigation (FBI). The investigation into a candidate's public record and professional abilities ordinarily is headed by high Justice Department officials, White House aides, or both, working together.

The investigatory process may be preliminary in nature when the object is to identify potential candidates and consider their relative merits based on information already known or readily available. The investigations become more intensive as the list is narrowed. The object then becomes to learn as much as possible about the prospective nominees—to accurately gauge their qualifications and their compatibility with the President's specific requirements for a nominee, and, simultaneously, to flag anything in their backgrounds that might be disqualifying or jeopardize their chances for Senate confirmation. For help in evaluating the backgrounds of Court candidates, Presidents sometimes also have enlisted the assistance of private lawyers,[43] legal scholars,[44] or the American Bar Association (ABA).[45] Near the culmination of this investigative effort, the President might want to personally meet with one or more of the candidates before finally deciding whom to nominate.[46]

During the pre-nomination phase, Presidents vary in the degree to which they publicly reveal the names of individuals under consideration for the Court. Sometimes, Presidents seek to keep confidential the identity of their Court candidates. Such secrecy may allow a President to reflect on the qualifications of prospective nominees, and the background investigations to proceed, away from the glare of publicity, news media coverage, and outside political pressures. Other times, the White House may, at least in the early pre-nomination stage, reveal the names of Supreme Court candidates being considered. Such openness may be intended to serve various purposes—among them, to test public or congressional reaction to potential nominees, please political constituencies who would identify with identified candidates, or demonstrate the President's determination to conduct a comprehensive search for the most qualified person available.

An Administration, of course, need not wait until a vacancy occurs on the Court to begin investigating the backgrounds of potential nominees. Immediately after President George W. Bush was sworn into office in 2001, according to a recent book on Supreme Court nominations, "his staff began putting together a list of potential nominees and conducting extensive background research on them." The book continued:

> Officials believed [Chief Justice William H.] Rehnquist was likely to retire in the summer of 2001, and they were determined to be ready. Each young lawyer in the White House counsel's office, most of whom had clerked on the Supreme Court, was assigned a candidate and made responsible for writing a lengthy report about him or her. In the late spring, then- White House counsel Alberto Gonzalez and his deputy Tim Flanigan began secretly interviewing some of those possible replacements.
>
> The advance work was designed to ensure that George W. Bush would be prepared when a justice stepped down.... The early in-depth research and interviews with prospective nominees were important in ensuring Bush would have coolheaded advice, removed from any external political pressure to select a particular nominee in the hours after a retirement.[47]

Speed with Which President Selects Nominees

When a Supreme Court vacancy occurs, Presidents sometimes move quickly, selecting their nominee within a week of the vacancy being announced.[48] A President may be well positioned to make a quick announcement when a retiring Justice alerts the President beforehand (thus giving the President lead time, before the vacancy occurs, to consider whom to nominate as a successor). Even when receiving no advance warning from an outgoing Justice, the President may already have in hand a "short list," prepared precisely for the event of a Court vacancy, of persons already evaluated and acceptable to the President for the appointment. If the President has a strong personal preference for a particular individual, nominating the person quickly preempts the issue of whether someone else should be nominated. Rather than focus on a range of individuals who should be considered for the Supreme Court, the appointment process moves to the next stage, to the question of whether that individual should be confirmed.

Presidents also might be moved to nominate quickly in order to minimize the time during which there is a vacancy on the Court. If an actual vacancy is suddenly created—for example, due to an unexpected retirement, resignation, or death of a Justice—a President, as well as Members of the Senate, might be eager to bring the Court back to full strength as soon as possible. A similar sense of urgency might be felt if a Justice has announced the intention to step down from the Court by a date certain in the near future.

Selecting a Supreme Court nominee quickly, however, may sometimes have drawbacks. A President may be accused of charging ahead with a nominee without having first adequately consulted with the Senate, or without having taken the time necessary to determine who really would make the best nominee. Also, quick announcements might not allow time for the FBI to conduct a comprehensive background investigation prior to nomination, leaving open the possibility of unfavorable information about the nominee coming to light later.[49]

The speed with which a President chooses a nominee also, as noted above, can be affected by when a seat on the Court is vacated. Sometimes, Justices might announce their retirement when the Court concludes its annual term, in late June or early July, giving the President little or no advance notice. In such situations, a President might decide to nominate quickly, to allow the Senate confirmation process to begin as quickly as possible. A swiftly made nomination, in such a circumstance, affords the Senate Judiciary Committee and the Senate as long as three months (July through September) in which to consider the nomination before the start of the Court's term in early October, thereby increasing the chances of the Court being at full nine-member strength when it reconvenes.

The President, however, is not obligated to nominate quickly, and other considerations might provide reasons for not doing so. For instance, from the President's standpoint, a nomination made in late June or early July, might, if followed by the scheduling of confirmation hearings by the Judiciary Committee as late as September, afford too much time in between (in July and August) for the nominee to be exposed to potential criticism by Senate or other opponents. A desire to minimize this exposure time for the nominee might cause a President to consider nominating later in the summer, putting more of the onus to act expeditiously on the Senate, if the Court is to be back at full strength when it reconvenes in October.

Sometimes, when Justices give advance notice of their intention to retire, Presidents might be under relatively little pressure to nominate quickly. In the spring of 1993, for example, Justice Byron R. White announced he would step down when the Court adjourned for the summer. His advance notice gave President Clinton and the Senate together more than six months in which, respectively, to nominate and confirm a successor before the beginning of the Court's next term in October.[50] A year later, in the spring of 1994, Justice Harry A. Blackmun announced his intention to retire at the end of the Court term then in progress, again affording the President and the Senate ample time to appoint a successor to a retiring Justice before the start of the next Court term.[51]

Presidents also may have considerable latitude in deciding when to nominate if an outgoing Justice schedules his or her retirement to take effect only when a successor is confirmed or assumes office. The most recent instance of that occurred when Justice Sandra Day O'Connor, in a July 1, 2005, letter to President George W. Bush, announced her decision to retire from the Court "effective upon the nomination and confirmation" of her successor.[52] At the announcement of Justice O'Connor's retirement, President Bush declared he would "choose a nominee in a timely manner" so that the nominee would receive a Senate hearing and confirmation vote "before the new Supreme Court term begins."[53] Within three weeks he announced his selection of John G. Roberts Jr. to succeed Justice O'Connor.[54] The conditional nature of Justice O'Connor's planned retirement, however, meant that her seat on the Court would be occupied when the Court convened for its October 2005 term, whether or not her successor were confirmed by then.

Ultimately, Justice O'Connor remained on the Court for four months of the new Court term, retiring only on January 31, 2006, when the third person nominated by President Bush to succeed her, Samuel A. Alito Jr., was confirmed by the Senate. During the months that Justice O'Connor remained on the Court, awaiting the confirmation of her successor, the Associate Justice nomination of John G. Roberts Jr. was withdrawn so that President Bush could nominate Roberts to be Chief Justice (following the death of Chief Justice Rehnquist on September 3, 2005); a second nomination to succeed Justice O'Connor, that of White House Counsel Harriet E. Miers, was made, only to be withdrawn three weeks later; and, on November 10, 2005, a third person, Samuel A. Alito Jr., was nominated to succeed Justice O'Connor. For a President, the need to select an Associate Justice nominee might be seen as less urgent than the appointment of a Chief Justice, particularly if, as was the case in 2005, the Chief Justice position is actually vacant and the Associate Justice vacancy is not actual, but prospective.

Recess Appointments to the Court

On 12 occasions in our nation's history (most of them in the 19th century), Presidents have made temporary appointments to the Supreme Court without submitting nominations to the Senate. These occurred when Presidents exercised their power under the Constitution to make "recess appointments" when the Senate was not in session.[55] Historically, when recesses between sessions of the Senate were much longer than they are today, "recess appointments" served the purpose of averting long vacancies on the Court when the Senate was unavailable to confirm a President's appointees. The terms of these "recess appointments," however, were limited, expiring at the end of the next session of Congress (unlike the lifetime appointments Court appointees receive when nominated and then confirmed by the Senate). Despite the temporary nature of these appointments, every person appointed during a recess of the Senate, except one, ultimately received a lifetime appointment to the Court after being nominated by the President and confirmed by the Senate.[56]

The last President to make recess appointments to the Court was Dwight D. Eisenhower. Of the five persons whom he nominated to the Court, three first received recess appointments and served as Justices before being confirmed—Earl Warren (as Chief Justice) in 1953, William Brennan in 1956, and Potter Stewart in 1958. President Eisenhower's recess appointments, however, generated controversy, prompting the Senate in 1960, voting closely along party lines, to pass a resolution expressing opposition to Supreme Court recess appointments in the future.[57]

While President Eisenhower's were the most recent recess appointments to the Supreme Court, recess appointments to the lower federal courts, since the late 1960s, also have become relatively rare. A President's constitutional power to make judicial recess appointments was upheld by a federal court in 1985[58] and again in 2004.[59] Such appointments, when they do occur, may cause controversy, in large part because they bypass the Senate and its "advice and consent" role. Because of the criticisms of judicial recess appointments in recent decades, the long passage of time since the last Supreme Court recess appointment, and the relatively short duration of contemporary Senate recesses (which arguably undercuts the need for recess appointments to the Court), a President in the 21st century might hesitate to make a recess appointment to the Court and do so only under the most unusual of circumstances.[60]

Consideration by the Senate Judiciary Committee

Historical Background

While the Constitution of the United States assigns explicit roles in the Supreme Court appointment process only to the President and the Senate,[61] the Senate Judiciary Committee, throughout much of our nation's history, has also played an important, intermediary role. From 1816, when the Judiciary Committee was created, until 1868, more than two-thirds of nominations to the Supreme Court were referred to the committee, in each case by motion. In 1868, the Senate determined, as a general rule, that all nominations should automatically be referred to appropriate standing committees.[62] Since then, almost all Supreme Court nominations (87 of 94) have been referred to the committee.[63]

An important exception to the practice of referring Supreme Court nominees to the Judiciary Committee, however, usually has been made for nominees who, at the time of their nomination, were current or former Members of the U.S. Senate. These nominees benefitted from "the unwritten rule of the all but automatic approval of senatorial colleagues,"[64] with the Senate moving quickly to confirm without first referring the nominations to committee.[65] The most recent demonstration of this "unwritten rule" occurred on June 12, 1941. On that day, President Franklin D. Roosevelt submitted three Supreme Court nominations to the Senate, those of Associate Justice Harlan F. Stone to be Chief Justice, Senator James F. Byrnes (D-SC) to be Associate Justice, and Robert H. Jackson to be Associate Justice. The Stone and Jackson nominations were both referred to the Senate Judiciary Committee, which held one day of public hearings on the former and four days of hearings on the latter, before reporting each favorably to the Senate. The overall time that elapsed between nomination and confirmation was 15 days for Stone and 25 days for Jackson.[66]

The Byrnes nomination, by contrast, was given expedited treatment by the Senate since the nominee was a Member of that body. The Senate considered and confirmed Senator Byrnes to the Court on the very day his nomination was received without referral of the nomination to the Judiciary Committee. When the Byrnes nomination was laid before the Senate, Senator Carter Glass (D-VA) moved that "the nomination of our colleague ... be now considered without reference to committee." In immediate response, Senator Charles L. McNary (R-OR) stated that "it has been the unbroken custom to adopt such a proposal as that made by the eminent Senator from Virginia, and I join him in his motion." The motion to consider the nomination without reference to committee was then seconded by the chair of the Judiciary Committee, Senator Frederick Van Nuys (D-IN). Moments later, the Senate confirmed the nomination by unanimous consent.[67]

The only instance since the Byrnes nomination in 1941 of a sitting Senator being named to the Court occurred in 1945. In this episode, the nomination of Senator Harold H. Burton (R-OH), unlike that of Byrnes, was referred to the Judiciary Committee. Referral to the committee, however, did not signal any problems ahead for Senator Burton, as the committee's handling of his nomination was swift and pro forma: A day after the nomination's receipt in the Senate, the committee, without holding a hearing, unanimously reported it to the Senate, where hours later it was confirmed by unanimous consent.[68]

The decades since 1945 have yet to test whether there remains an enduring Senate tradition of bypassing the Judiciary Committee when the Supreme Court nominee is a sitting U.S. Senator— as no President since then has nominated a sitting Senator. The last *former* Senator to be nominated to the Court, in 1949, was Judge Sherman Minton of Indiana. (After defeat for re-election to the Senate in 1940, Minton had been appointed by President Franklin D. Roosevelt to a federal appellate court judgeship.) In this instance, Senate tradition was not adhered to: The Supreme Court nomination of the former Senator was referred to the Judiciary Committee, which held a hearing on the nomination before reporting it favorably, by a vote of 9-2. On the Senate floor, confirmation came not by unanimous consent or voice vote but by a roll-call vote that was not unanimous (48-16).[69]

During the 19th century, the Judiciary Committee routinely considered Supreme Court nominations behind closed doors, with its deliberations during the 20th century gradually becoming more public in nature. According to one expert source,[70] the earliest Supreme Court confirmation hearings held in open session were those in 1916 for the nomination of Louis D. Brandeis to be an Associate Justice. In 1925, Harlan F. Stone became the first Supreme Court nominee to appear in person and testify at his confirmation hearings.[71]

Neither the Brandeis nor the Stone hearings, however, served as binding precedents. Public confirmation hearings for Supreme Court nominations did not become a regular practice of the Judiciary Committee until the late 193 0s. Of the five Supreme Court nominees after Stone in 1925, three (Charles Evans Hughes for Chief Justice in 1930, Owen J. Roberts for Associate Justice in 1930, and Senator Hugo C. Black for Associate Justice in 1937) did not receive confirmation hearings. Then, starting with the nomination of Stanley

F. Reed in 1938, every Supreme Court nominee, except for two in the 1940s[72] and two in 2005,[73] would receive a hearing. Initially, however, the hearings in the 1930s and 1940s were usually brief and perfunctory, held only long enough to accommodate the small number of witnesses who wanted to testify against a nominee.[74]

Also, notwithstanding Stone's appearance at his hearings in 1925, the Judiciary Committee, over the next 30 years, usually declined to invite Supreme Court nominees to testify if a confirmation hearing were held;[75] hence, as recently as 1954, Earl Warren did not appear at his confirmation hearings to be Chief Justice. However, hearings in 1955 on the Supreme Court nomination of John M. Harlan marked the beginning of a practice, continuing to the present, of each Court nominee testifying before the Judiciary Committee.[76] In 1981, Supreme Court confirmation hearings were opened to gavel-to-gavel television coverage for the first time, when the committee instituted the practice at the confirmation hearings for nominee Sandra Day O'Connor.[77]

Whereas, historically, nominees were routinely uninvolved in the appointment process, they have now become active participants. Indeed, at hearings, a nominee's demeanor, responsiveness and knowledge of the law may be crucial in influencing the committee members' and other Senators' votes on confirmation.

Another important historical trend has involved the pace and thoroughness of the Judiciary Committee in acting on Supreme Court nominations. Throughout the second half of the 19th century and the first half of the 20th century, it was the standard practice, unless Senators at the outset found a nominee to be objectionable for some reason, for the committee to act on and dispose of a nomination within days of receiving it. In recent decades, by contrast, the committee has tended to proceed much more deliberately, with its official involvement in the appointment process now usually measured in weeks or months.[78]

Since the late 1960s, the Judiciary Committee's consideration of a Supreme Court nominee almost always has consisted of three distinct stages—a pre-hearing investigative stage, followed by public hearings, and concluding with a committee decision on what recommendation to make to the full Senate.

Pre-Hearing Stage

Immediately upon the President's announcement of a nominee, the Judiciary Committee initiates its own intensive investigation into the nominee's background. One primary source of information is a committee questionnaire to which the nominee responds in writing.[79] Confidential FBI reports on the nominee are another important information source. These are available only to committee members and a small number of designated staff under strict security procedures designed to prevent unauthorized disclosure. Also, independently of the FBI, committee staff conduct their own confidential investigations into the nominee's background.

If the nominee's background includes prior service in the federal executive branch, the Judiciary Committee as a whole, or some of its members, also can be expected to seek access to records of the nominee's written work product from that service. Sometimes, however, a President might resist such requests, citing the need to protect the confidentiality of advice provided, or decisions made, by the nominee while having served within an Administration—and typically invoking an "executive privilege" or attorney-client privilege to support his refusal to make such information available to the Judiciary Committee.[80] In such an event, committee members or their staff might then devote a significant amount of time, prior to confirmation hearings, to identifying and justifying disclosure of specific kinds of documents that would aid the committee in making a more informed evaluation of the nominee—as well as to examining whatever documents are eventually released. In some cases, the committee may be in a position to exert leverage over an Administration, particularly when a majority of the committee's members are insistent that at least some executive branch documents be released before the committee will act on the nomination. This, a CRS report notes, was the case in 1986, when the Judiciary Committee prepared to consider the nomination of William H. Rehnquist to be Chief Justice.

> During the confirmation proceeding for the elevation of Justice Rehnquist to be Chief Justice, the Judiciary Committee sought documents that he had authored on controversial subjects when he headed DOJ's Office of Legal Counsel. President Reagan asserted executive privilege, claiming the need to protect the candor and confidentiality of the legal advice submitted to Presidents and their assistants. But with opponents of Rehnquist [in the Judiciary Committee] gearing up to issue a subpoena, the nomination of not

only Rehnquist but that of Antonin Scalia to be an Associate Justice, whose nominations were to be voted on in tandem, were in jeopardy. President Reagan agreed to allow the Committee access to a smaller number of documents, and Rehnquist and Scalia were ultimately confirmed.[81]

Meanwhile, the nominee, in accordance with longstanding tradition, visits Capitol Hill to pay "courtesy calls" on individual Senators in their offices. For Senators not on the Judiciary Committee, that may be the only opportunity to converse in person with the nominee before voting on his or her confirmation to the Court. Senators may use these meetings to gain firsthand impressions of the nominee and to discuss with the nominee issues that are important to them in the context of the nomination.[82]

Also during the pre-hearing stage, the nominee is evaluated by the American Bar Association's Standing Committee on the Federal Judiciary.[83] The stated function of the ABA committee is to impartially evaluate judicial nominees. Each evaluation, according to the committee, concentrates on the candidate's "integrity, professional competence and judicial temperament,"[84] with the goal being "to support and encourage the selection of the best qualified persons for the federal judiciary."[85] At the culmination of its evaluation, the ABA committee votes on whether to rate a nominee "well-qualified," "qualified," or "not qualified." The rating of the ABA committee is then reported to each member of the Senate Judiciary Committee, as well as to the White House, the Department of Justice, and the nominee.[86]

For the most part, from its inception in the late 1940s, and continuing through the next three decades, the ABA committee evaluated Supreme Court nominees, as well as nominees to lower court judgeships, with bipartisan support in the Senate. In the 1980s and 1990s, however, the committee came under increasing criticism from some Senators, who questioned its impartiality and the usefulness of its nominee evaluations to the Judiciary Committee.[87] Among the critics was Senator Orrin G. Hatch (R-UT), who, in 1997, as chair of the Judiciary Committee, announced that, during his chairmanship, the ABA committee would no longer be accorded an "officially sanctioned role" in the judicial confirmation process.[88] However, in 2001, the Judiciary Committee's next chair, Senator Patrick J. Leahy (D-VT), restored to the ABA committee a quasi-official evaluating role, stating that the Judiciary Committee's Democratic members would oppose votes on any of President George W. Bush's judicial nominees who were not first reviewed by the ABA committee.[89]

Notwithstanding past criticisms of it, and variations in the recognition afforded it by chairs of the Judiciary Committee, the ABA committee has continued, in recent Congresses, to appear on a regular basis before the Judiciary Committee, under both Republican and Democratic chairs. It has done so, for instance, when testifying on lower court judicial nominees who have received "Not Qualified" ratings. Also, in keeping with longstanding practice, the ABA committee chair was the first public witness to testify at the two most recent Supreme Court confirmation hearings in 2005 and 2006—to explain the ABA committee's rating of nominees John G. Roberts Jr. and Samuel A. Alito Jr., respectively.[90] At the Alito hearings, the then-chair of the Judiciary Committee, Senator Arlen Specter (R-PA), observed that, in receiving the testimony of outside witnesses at Supreme Court confirmation hearings, "our tradition is to hear first from the American Bar Association and their evaluation of the judicial nominee."[91]

Meanwhile, it is common, well before the start of confirmation hearings, for public debate to begin on a nominee's qualifications and on the meaning of the nomination for the future of the Court. Much of this debate is waged by commentators in the news media and increasingly, in recent years, on Internet sites, and by advocacy groups that actively support or oppose a nominee.[92] Senators, too, sometimes contribute to this debate in Senate floor statements or other public remarks. Moreover, if a nominee is not quickly selected, groups who see their interests to be at stake by a new Court appointment can be expected to begin mobilizing members, or seeking to affect public or Senate opinion, before the President selects a nominee. Their purpose in doing might be to influence the President's choice or to galvanize the groups' members and political allies in anticipation of whomever the President chooses.[93]

If, ultimately, the President's choice of a nominee proves to be divisive, the pre-hearing phase will be of strategic concern both to those groups which support and those which oppose the nominee. During this phase, a political analyst has noted, "both sides will move quickly to try to define the nominee."[94] The analysis, published in July 2005, only days after Justice Sandra Day O'Connor announced her intention to retire, considered what might happen if President George W. Bush's choice to succeed Justice O'Connor created an immediate polarization in the Senate along party lines. In that event, it predicted the following scenario prior to the nominee's confirmation hearings:

> First impressions are lasting impressions. If Republicans can create a positive image of a Bush Supreme Court nominee in the public's mind right out of the gate, that could help the nominee withstand later efforts by critics to portray him or her as an extremist. Conversely, if Democrats can quickly paint the president's choice as ideologically driven and far out of the mainstream, that could be a deathblow.[95]

However, even if a nominee is not a "consensus" choice attracting immediate support across the political spectrum, the pre-hearing stage will not necessarily be marked by sharp polarization in the Senate or by the immediate emergence of Senate opposition. Such deep division, for instance, was absent when President Bush, on July 19, 2005, announced his selection of U.S. appellate court judge John G. Roberts Jr. to succeed the retiring Justice O'Connor. While "[l]iberal advocacy groups immediately assailed Roberts for his positions on abortion and other issues," and "Republican senators quickly rallied behind Roberts," Senate Democrats withheld immediate criticism of the nominee—reportedly out of concern about falling into what the Senate Democratic leader, according to aides, "considered a Republican trap of condemning a nominee before hearings...."[96]

As confirmation hearings approach, Judiciary Committee members and staff closely study the public record and investigative information compiled on the nominee,[97] and with the benefit of such research, they prepare questions to pose at the hearings. Sometimes committee members indicate in advance, either publicly or by communicating directly with the nominee, the kind of questions they intend to ask at the hearings.[98]

For his or her part, the nominee also intensively prepares for the hearings, focusing particularly on questions of law and policy likely to be raised by committee members. The Administration assists the nominee in this effort by providing legal background materials and by conducting mock hearing practice sessions for the nominee. At these sessions—also called "murder boards," because of "their grueling demands on a judicial nominee"[99]—the nominee is questioned on the full range of legal and constitutional issues that Senators on the Judiciary Committee can be expected to raise at the nominee's confirmation hearings.[100]

Hearings

A confirmation hearing typically begins with a statement by the chair of the Judiciary Committee welcoming the nominee and outlining how the hearing will proceed.[101] Other members of the committee follow with opening statements, and a panel of "presenters" introduces the nominee to the committee.[102] It is then the nominee's turn to make an opening statement, after which begins the principal business of the hearing—the questioning of the nominee by Senators serving on the Judiciary Committee. Typically, the chair begins the questioning, followed by the ranking minority member and then the rest of the committee in descending order of seniority, alternating between majority and minority members, with a uniform time limit for each Senator during each round. When the first round of questioning has been completed, the committee begins a second round, which may be followed by more rounds, at the discretion of the committee chair.[103]

In recent decades, most nominees have undergone rigorous questioning in varying subject areas. They have been queried, as a matter of course, about their legal qualifications, private backgrounds, and earlier actions as public figures. Other questions have focused on social and political issues, the Constitution, particular Court rulings, current constitutional controversies, constitutional values, judicial philosophy, and the analytical approach a nominee might use in deciding issues and cases.[104] To many Senators, eliciting testimony from the nominee may be seen as an important way to gain insight into the nominee's professional qualifications, temperament, and character. Some Senators, as well, may hope to glean from the nominee's responses signs of how the nominee, if confirmed to the Court, might be expected to rule on issues of particular concern to the Senators.[105]

For his or her part, however, a nominee might sometimes be reluctant to answer certain questions that are posed at confirmation hearings.[106] A nominee might decline to answer for fear of appearing to make commitments on issues that later could come before the Court.[107] A nominee also might be concerned that the substance of candid responses to certain questions could displease some Senators and thus put the nominee's chances for confirmation in jeopardy.

For their part, committee members may differ in their assessments of a nominee's stated reasons for refusing to answer certain questions.[108] Some may be sympathetic and consider a nominee's refusal to discuss certain matters as of no relevance to his or her fitness for appointment, or as illustrative of a commendable inclination not to be "pinned down" on current legal controversies. Others, however, may consider a nominee's views on certain subjects as important to assessing the nominee's fitness and hence regard unresponsiveness to questions on these subjects as sufficient reason to vote against confirmation.[109] Protracted questioning, occurring over several days of hearings, is likely, especially if a nominee is relatively controversial or is perceived by committee members to be evasive or insincere in responding to certain questions, or if Senators perceive certain issues to merit extended discussion.

For members of the Judiciary Committee, questioning of the nominee may serve various purposes. As already noted, for Senators who are undecided about the nominee, the hearings may shed light on the nominee's fitness, and hence on how they should vote. Other Senators, as the hearings begin, may already be "reasonably certain about voting to confirm the nominee," yet "also remain reasonably open to counter-evidence," and thus use the hearings "to pursue a line of questioning designed to probe the validity of this initial favorable predisposition."[110] Still others, however, may come to the hearings "having already decided how they will vote on the nomination" and, accordingly, use their questioning of the nominee to try "to secure or defeat the nomination."[111] For some Senators, the hearings may be a vehicle through which to impress certain values or concerns upon a nominee, in the hope of influencing how he or she might approach issues later as a Justice.[112] The hearings also may represent to some Senators an opportunity to draw the public's attention to certain issues, to advocate their policy preferences, or to associate themselves with concern about certain problems. Senators, it has also been noted, "may play multiple roles in any given hearings."[113]

After questioning the nominee has been completed, the committee, in subsequent days of hearings, also hears testimony from public witnesses. As stated earlier, among the first to testify in recent decades has been the chair of the ABA's Standing Committee on the Federal Judiciary, who explains the committee's rating of a nominee. Other witnesses ordinarily include spokespersons for advocacy groups which support or oppose a nominee.

In a practice instituted in 1992, the Judiciary Committee also has conducted a closed-door session with each Court nominee. This session is held to address any questions about the nominee's background that confidential investigations might have brought to the committee's attention. In announcing this procedure in 1992, the then-chair of the committee, Senator Joseph R. Biden Jr. (D-DE), explained that such a hearing would be conducted "in all cases, even when there are no major investigative issues to be resolved so that the holding of such a hearing cannot be taken to demonstrate that the committee has received adverse confidential information about the nomination."[114]

The first such closed-door session was held for Supreme Court nominee Ruth Bader Ginsburg in 1993, separate from public hearings that the committee held on her nomination. Most recently, such sessions were held in 2005 and 2006 for nominees John G. Roberts Jr. and Samuel A. Alito Jr. In each case, a very brief executive session was held between the end of the nominee's public testimony and the start of outside witness testimony.[115]

Reporting the Nomination

Usually within a week of the end of hearings, the Judiciary Committee meets in open session to determine what recommendation to "report" to the full Senate. The committee may report favorably, negatively, or make no recommendation at all. A report with a negative recommendation or no recommendation permits a nomination to go forward, while alerting the Senate that a substantial number of committee members have reservations about the nominee.

If a majority of its members oppose confirmation, the committee technically may decide not to report a nomination, to prevent the full Senate from considering the nominee. However, since its creation in 1816, the Judiciary Committee's almost invariable practice has been to report even those Supreme Court nominations that were opposed by a committee majority,[116] thus allowing the full Senate to make the final decision on whether the nominee should be confirmed.[117] This committee tradition was reaffirmed in June 2001 by the committee's then-chair, Senator Patrick J. Leahy (D-VT), and its then-ranking member, Senator Orrin G. Hatch (R-UT), in a June 29, 2001, letter to Senate colleagues. The committee's "traditional practice," their letter stated,

> ... has been to report Supreme Court nominees to the Senate once the Committee has completed its considerations. This has been true even in cases where Supreme Court nominees were opposed by a majority of the Judiciary Committee.
>
> We both recognize and have every intention of following the practices and precedents of the committee and the Senate when considering Supreme Court nominees.[118]

In recent decades, reporting to the Senate frequently, if not always, has included a printed committee report.[119] Prepared behind closed doors, after the committee has voted on the nominee, the printed report presents in a single volume the views of committee members supporting a nominee's confirmation as well as "all supplemental, minority, or additional views ... submitted by the time of the filing of the report...."[120] No Senate committee, however, is normally obliged to transmit a printed report to the Senate. Instead, the chair of the Judiciary Committee may simply file a one-page document reporting a nomination to the Senate and recommending whether the nomination should be confirmed.

A printed report, it can be argued, is valuable in providing for Senators not on the Judiciary Committee a review, in one volume, of all of the reasons that the committee's members cite for voting in favor or against a nominee.[121] A written report, however, might not always be considered a necessary reference for the Senate as a whole. For instance, in some cases, Senators not on the Judiciary Committee might believe they have received adequate information about a nominee from other sources, such as from news media reports or gavel-to-gavel video coverage of the nominee's confirmation hearings. Further, preparation of a written report will mean additional days for a nomination to stay with the committee before it can be reported to the Senate.[122] In some situations, this might be viewed as creating unnecessary delay in the confirmation process, particularly if there is a desire to fill a Court vacancy as quickly as possible.[123]

The Senate usually, but not always, has agreed with Judiciary Committee recommendations that a Supreme Court nominee be confirmed.[124] Historically, negative committee reports, or reports without recommendation, have been precursors to nominations encountering substantial opposition in the full Senate, although a few of these nominations have eventually been confirmed by narrow margins.[125]

Senate Debate and Confirmation Vote

Bringing the Nomination to the Floor[126]

After the Judiciary Committee has reported a nomination, it is placed on the Executive Calendar and assigned a Calendar number by the executive clerk of the Senate.[127] As with other nominations listed in the Executive Calendar, information about a Supreme Court nomination includes the name and office of the nominee; the name of the previous holder of the office; whether the committee reported the nomination favorably, unfavorably, or without recommendation; and, if there is a printed report, the report number.[128] Business on the Executive Calendar, which consists of treaties and nominations, is considered in executive session.[129] Unless voted otherwise by the Senate, executive sessions are open to the public.[130] Floor debate on a Supreme Court nomination, in contemporary practice, invariably has been conducted in public session, open to the public and press and, since 1986, to live nationwide television coverage.[131]

Consideration of a nomination is scheduled by the majority leader, in consultation with the minority leader and with all interested Senators. At the time agreed on, or at the majority leader's initiative, the Senate proceeds to executive session, either by a motion or by unanimous consent. In recent decades, the almost invariable practice in calling up a Supreme Court nomination has been for the majority leader to ask for unanimous consent that the Senate consider the nomination. The leader may ask for unanimous consent to proceed to executive session to consider the nomination immediately,[132] or at some specified date and time in the future.[133]

Unanimous consent requests also may include a limit on the time that will be allowed for debate and specify the date and time on which the Senate will vote on a nomination.[134] Typically, the amount of time agreed upon for debate is divided evenly between the majority and minority parties, who usually have as their respective floor managers the chair and ranking minority member of the Judiciary Committee. If agreed to, a time limit on debate, with a date and time set for Senate vote, forecloses the use of unlimited debate by opponents of the nomination—a tactic known, in Senate procedural parlance, as the filibuster. Conversely, if the Senate agrees by unanimous consent to consider a nomination, but does not provide for a time limit on debate or specify when, or under what circumstances, a Senate vote will take place, unlimited debate is possible, although not necessarily inevitable.[135]

When unanimous consent to call up a nomination cannot be secured, a procedural alternative is to make a *motion* that the Senate proceed to consider the nomination. Such a motion may be made while the Senate is in executive or legislative session. If the majority leader moves to consider the nomination during executive session, the motion is debatable under Senate rules."[136] Closing debate on the motion, in turn, may require the Senate to invoke cloture by an affirmative vote of three-fifths of the entire Senate membership (60

Senators if there are no vacancies).[137] A majority leader today is unlikely to make such a motion while in executive session since the motion is debatable.

The debatable nature of a motion to consider, when made in executive session, was demonstrated in 1968, when the nomination of Associate Justice Abe Fortas to be Chief Justice was brought to the Senate floor. The episode marked the most recent Senate proceedings in which a *motion* was made to proceed to consider a Supreme Court nomination while the Senate was in *executive* session. Significant opposition within the Senate to the Fortas nomination raised the theoretical possibility of two filibusters being mounted—the first against the motion to consider, and then (if Fortas supporters were successful in ending debate on the first filibuster) a second, against the nomination itself.[138] The second filibuster, however, failed to materialize when the Senate declined, by the super-majority vote required, to close debate on the motion to consider.[139]

A motion to consider a nomination, however, may also be made while the Senate is in *legislative* session, and such a motion is not debatable. Since 1980, the Senate precedent has been explicitly established that when the Senate is in legislative session, a non-debatable motion may be made to go into executive session to take up a specified nomination.[140] If adhered to, the precedent, according to one congressional scholar, would limit a potential filibuster to the nomination itself.[141]

As discussed below,[142] the most recent instance in which Senate opponents of a Supreme Court nomination sought to block, or indefinitely delay, a vote on confirmation involved Associate Justice nominee Samuel A. Alito Jr., in January 2006. However, the possibility of two filibusters against the Alito nomination—namely, one against proceeding to consideration and a second against a vote on confirmation—was precluded the day after the nomination was reported to the Senate. On that day, January 25, 2006, the Senate, while in legislative session, agreed by unanimous consent to immediately proceed to executive session to consider the Alito nomination. From that point forward, debate in the Senate concerning the nomination had moved beyond the question of whether to consider and on to the question of whether to confirm Under these circumstances, Senate approval of only one cloture motion, not two, was required to end debate and bring the nomination to a confirmation vote.[143]

Criteria Used to Evaluate Nominees

Once the Senate begins debate on a Supreme Court nomination, many Senators typically will take part in the debate. Some, in their remarks, underscore the importance of the Senate's "advice and consent" role, and the consequent responsibility to carefully determine the qualifications of a nominee before voting to confirm.[144] Invariably, each Senator who takes the floor states his or her reasons for voting in favor of or against a nominee's confirmation.

The criteria used to evaluate a Supreme Court nominee are a personal, very individual matter for each Senator.[145] In their floor remarks, some Senators may cite a nominee's professional qualifications or character as the key criterion,[146] others may stress the importance of the nominee's judicial philosophy or views on constitutional issues,[147] while still others may indicate that they are influenced in varying degrees by all of these criteria.[148]

In recent decades, the Senate debate on virtually every Supreme Court nomination has focused to some extent on the nominee's judicial philosophy, ideology, constitutional values, or known positions on specific legal controversies. Many highly controversial decisions of the Court in recent decades have been closely decided, by 5-4 votes, appearing to underscore a longstanding philosophical or ideological divide in the Court between its more so-called liberal and so-called conservative members. A new appointee to the Court, Senators recognize, could have a potentially decisive impact on the Court's currently perceived ideological "balance" and on whether past rulings of the Court will be upheld, modified, or overturned in the future.[149] Announcements by the Court of 5-4 decisions, a journalist covering the Court in 2001 wrote, had "become routine, a familiar reminder of how much the next appointment to the court will matter."[150]

Senators sometimes will indicate in their floor statements whether they believe the views of a particular nominee, although not in complete accord with their own views, nonetheless, fall within a broad range of acceptable legal thinking.[151] Senators' concerns with a nominee's judicial philosophy or ideology may become heightened, and their positions more polarized relative to other Senators', if a nominee's philosophical orientation is seen as controversial, or if the President is perceived to have made the nomination with the specific intention of changing the Court's ideological balance.[152]

Other factors also may figure importantly into a Senator's confirmation decisions. One, it has been suggested, is peer influence in the Senate.[153] Particularly influential, for instance, might be Senate colleagues who are championing a nominee or spearheading the opposition, or who played prominent roles in the Judiciary Committee hearings stage. Another consideration for Senators will be the views of their constituents, especially if many voters back home are thought to feel strongly about a nomination.[154] A third source of influence may be the views of a Senator's advisers, family, and friends, as well as the position taken on the nomination by advocacy groups that the Senator ordinarily trusts or looks to for perspective.[155]

Just as Presidents are assumed to do when considering prospective nominees for the Supreme Court, Senators may evaluate the suitability of a Supreme Court nominee according to whether certain groups, constituencies, or individuals with certain characteristics are adequately represented on the Court.[156] Among the representational criteria commonly considered have been the nominee's party affiliation, geographic origin, ethnicity, religion, and gender.[157]

When considering Supreme Court nominations, Senators may also take Senate institutional factors into account. For instance, the role, if any, that Senators from the home state of a nominee played in the nominee's selection, as well as their support for or opposition to the nominee, may be of interest to other Senators. At the same time, Senators may be interested in the extent to which the President, prior to selecting the nominee, sought advice from other quarters in the Senate—for instance, from Senate party leaders and from the chair, ranking minority member, and other Senators on the Judiciary Committee. A President's prior consultation with a wide range of Senators concerning a nominee may be a positive factor for other Members of the Senate, by virtue of conveying presidential respect for the role of Senate advice, as well as Senate consent, in the judicial appointments process.[158]

Sometimes, Senators may find themselves debating whether the Senate, in its "advice and consent" role, should defer to the President and give a nominee the "benefit of the doubt." This issue received particular attention during Senate consideration of the Supreme Court nomination of Clarence Thomas in 1991. In that debate, some Thomas supporters argued that the Senate, as a rule, should defer to the President's judgment concerning a nominee except when unfavorable information is presented overcoming the presumption in the nominee's favor.[159] Opponents, by contrast, rejected the notion that there was a presumption in favor of a Supreme Court nominee at the start of the confirmation process or that the President, in his selection of a nominee, is owed any special deference.[160]

That Senators continue to have differing views regarding appropriate evaluation criteria for Supreme Court nominees was apparent at Senate hearings on the judicial selection process held on June 26, 2001. At the hearings, a Senate Judiciary subcommittee examined the question of what role ideology should play in the selection and confirmation of federal judges.[161] In his opening remarks, the chair of the subcommittee, Senator Charles E. Schumer (D-NY), stated that it was clear that "the ideology of particular nominees often plays a significant role in the confirmation process." The current era, he said, "certainly justifies Senate opposition to judicial nominees whose views fall outside the mainstream and who have been selected in an attempt to further tilt the courts in an ideological direction."[162]

By contrast, Senator Orrin G. Hatch (R-UT), in testimony before the subcommittee, declared that there "are myriad reasons why political ideology has not been—and is not—an appropriate measure of judicial qualifications. Fundamentally," he continued, "the Senate's responsibility to provide advice and consent does not include an ideological litmus test because a nominee's personal opinions are largely irrelevant so long as the nominee can set those opinions aside and follow the law fairly and impartially as a judge."[163]

Filibusters and Motions to End Debate[164]

Senate rules place no limits on how long floor consideration of a nomination may last.[165] With time limits lacking, Senators opposing a Supreme Court nominee may seek, if they are so inclined, to use extended debate or delaying actions to postpone or prevent a vote from occurring. The use of dilatory actions for such a purpose is known as the filibuster.[166]

By the same token, however, supporters of a Court nomination have available to them a procedure for placing time limits on consideration of a matter—the motion to invoke cloture. When the Senate agrees to a cloture motion, further consideration of the matter being debated is limited to 30 hours. The majority required for cloture on most matters, including nominations, is three-fifths of the full membership of the Senate—60, if there are no vacancies.[167] By invoking cloture, the Senate ensures that a nomination may ultimately come to a vote and be decided by a voting majority.

Motions to bring debate on Supreme Court nominations to a close have been made on only four occasions.[168] The first use occurred in 1968, when Senate supporters of Justice Abe Fortas tried unsuccessfully to end debate on the motion to proceed to his nomination to be Chief Justice. After the motion was debated at length, the Senate failed to invoke cloture by a 45-43 vote,[169] prompting President Johnson to withdraw the nomination. (The 45 votes in favor of cloture fell far short of the super-majority required—then two-thirds of Senators present and voting, a quorum being present.) A cloture motion to end debate on a Court nomination occurred again in 1971, when the Senate considered the nomination of William H. Rehnquist to be an Associate Justice. Although the cloture motion failed by a 52-42 vote,[170] Rehnquist was confirmed later the same day.[171] In 1986, a cloture motion was filed on a third Supreme Court nomination, this time of sitting Associate Justice Rehnquist to be Chief Justice. Supporters of the nomination mustered more than the three-fifths majority needed to end debate (with the Senate voting for cloture 68-31),[172] and Justice Rehnquist subsequently was confirmed as Chief Justice.

A cloture motion was presented to end consideration of a Supreme Court nomination a fourth time, during Senate consideration of the nomination of Samuel A. Alito Jr. in January 2006. The motion was presented on January 26, after two days of Senate floor debate on the nomination.[173] On January 30, the Senate voted to invoke cloture by a 72-25 vote,[174] and the next day it confirmed the Alito nomination by a vote of 5 8-42.

As one news analysis observed, Senators "are traditionally hesitant to filibuster judicial nominations."[175] Indicative of this, the article noted, was the fact that some of the "most divisive Supreme Court nominees in recent decades, including Associate Justice Clarence Thomas, have moved through the Senate without opponents resorting to that procedural weapon."[176] In 1991, five days of debate on the Thomas nomination concluded with a 52-48 confirmation vote. The 48 opposition votes would have been more than enough to defeat a cloture motion if one had been filed. In three earlier episodes, Senate opponents of Supreme Court nominations appear to have refrained from use of the filibuster, even though their numbers would have been sufficient to defeat a cloture motion. In 1969, 1970, and 1987 respectively, lengthy debate occurred on the unsuccessful nominations of Clement F. Haynsworth, G. Harrold Carswell, and Robert H. Bork. In none of these episodes, however, was a cloture motion filed, and in each case debate ended with a Senate vote rejecting the nomination.

Although use of the filibuster against Supreme Court nominations has been relatively rare in the past, the number of filibusters conducted or threatened against lower court nominations has increased in recent years. During the 108th Congress, 10 of President George W. Bush's 34 nominees to U.S. circuit court of appeals judgeships were blocked when motions to end debate on the nominations failed to gain passage in the Senate.[177] Several of these nominations, after resubmission by President Bush in the 109th Congress, again faced the prospect of being filibustered by Senate Democrats, to the displeasure of the Senate's Republican leadership.[178] In May 2005, leaders of the Senate's Republican majority announced their intention, if filibusters against nominations continued, to change the chamber's rules or precedents to require the vote of only a simple Senate majority to end Senate debate on judicial nominations.[179]

A Senate confrontation between the two parties over judicial filibusters was averted on May 23, 2005, when an agreement was reached by a coalition of seven Democratic and seven Republican Senators. As part of the agreement, the coalition's Democratic Senators pledged not to lend their support to filibusters against judicial nominations except under "extraordinary circumstances," while the Republican Senators in the coalition agreed not to support any change in the Senate rules to bar filibusters against judicial nominations, as long as the "spirit and continuing commitments made in this agreement" were kept by all of Senators in the coalition.[180]

In recent years, prior to the May 23, 2005 agreement, some Senators had raised the possibility of a filibuster being conducted against a future Supreme Court nomination, particularly if a vacancy on the Court occurred during the presidency of George W. Bush.[181] Subsequently, in November 2005, the selection by President Bush of Samuel A. Alito Jr. for the Court immediately raised the question of whether Senators likely to oppose Alito might also support a filibuster against his nomination.[182] Ultimately, during Senate floor consideration of the Alito nomination in January 2006, some Senators opposed to Alito did seek to prevent ending debate on his nomination.[183] The effort, however, proved unsuccessful. On January 30, 2006, the Senate voted 72-25 in favor of a motion to end debate on the Alito nomination, well in excess of the 60 needed for the motion to carry.[184] The next day the Senate voted to confirm Alito by a 58-42 vote. The 58-42 vote, a newspaper editorial observed, "allowed Judge Alito to become Justice Alito even though enough Democrats opposed the nomination to stop it with a filibuster."[185]

Voice Votes, Roll Calls, and Vote Margins

When floor debate on a nomination comes to a close, the presiding officer puts the question of confirmation to a vote. In doing so, the presiding officer typically states, "The question is, Will the Senate advise and consent to the nomination of [nominee's name] of [state of residence] to be an Associate Justice [or Chief Justice] on the Supreme Court?"[186] A roll-call vote to confirm requires a simple majority of Senators present and voting, a quorum being present.[187] Since 1967, every Senate vote on whether to confirm a Supreme Court nomination has been by roll call.[188] Prior to 1967, by contrast, fewer than half of all of Senate votes on whether to confirm nominees to the Court were by roll call, with the rest by voice vote.[189]

Historically, vote margins on the Supreme Court nominations have varied considerably. Some of the recorded votes, either confirming or rejecting a nomination, have been close.[190] Most votes, however, have been over whelmingly in favor of confirmation.[191]

For roll-call votes on Supreme Court nominations, the formal procedure by which Senators cast their votes on the floor has varied over the years. In recent decades prior to 1991, it was the usual practice for Senators, during the calling of the roll, to be free to come and go, and not have to be present in the Senate chamber for the entire calling of the roll. For the five most recent Supreme Court nominations, however, starting with nominee Clarence Thomas in 1991, the majority leader or the presiding officer, immediately prior to the calling of the roll, has asked all of the Senate's Members to remain seated at their desks during the entire vote—with each Senator rising and responding when his or her name is called. [192] Voting from the desk during roll calls is in keeping with a standing order of the Senate,[193] which rarely, however, is actually enforced;[194] nevertheless, the rule has been applied by Senate leaders, in recent years, to roll-call votes on Supreme Court nominations, to mark the special significance for the Senate of deciding whether to confirm an appointment to the nation's highest court.[195]

Reconsideration of the Confirmation Vote

After a Senate vote to confirm a Supreme Court nomination, a Senator who voted on the prevailing side may, under Senate Rule XXXI, move to reconsider the vote.[196] Under the rule, only one such motion to reconsider is in order on each nomination, and the tabling of the motion prevents any subsequent attempt to reconsider. The Senate typically deals with a motion to reconsider a Supreme Court confirmation in one of two ways. Immediately following the vote to confirm, a Senator may move to reconsider the vote, and the motion is promptly laid upon the table by unanimous consent.[197] Alternatively, well before the vote to confirm, in a unanimous consent agreement, the Senate may provide that, in the event of confirmation, the motion to reconsider be tabled.[198] The Senate, it should be noted, has never adopted a motion to reconsider a Supreme Court confirmation vote.

Nominations That Failed to Be Confirmed

Of the 158 nominations that have been made to the Supreme Court over the course of more than two centuries, 36 were not confirmed by the Senate. Of the 36 not confirmed, 11 were rejected by the Senate (all in roll-call votes), 11 were withdrawn by the President, and 14 lapsed at the end of a session of Congress without a Senate vote cast on whether to confirm.[199] The 36 nominations not confirmed by the Senate, a Congressional Research Service (CRS) report has found, represented 31 individuals, six of whom were later re-nominated and confirmed for positions on the Court. Of the other 25 nominees, four were nominated and failed confirmation more than once.[200] **Table 2**, in the following pages, provides information on the outcome of each of the 36 unconfirmed nominations.[201]

Various scholars, as well as the aforementioned CRS report,[202] have analyzed or provided a broad overview of factors associated with unsuccessful Supreme Court nominations.[203] In a history of Supreme Court appointments from Presidents Washington to Clinton, one scholar identified eight of the more "prominent reasons" why Supreme Court nominations were "rejected either outright or just simply were not acted upon by the Senate," listing these reasons as the following:

> (1) opposition to the nominating president, not necessarily the nominee; (2) the nominee's involvement with one or more contentious issues of public policy or, simply, opposition to the nominee's perceived jurisprudential or sociopolitical philosophy (i.e., politics); (3) opposition to the record of the incumbent Court, which, rightly or wrongly, the nominee presumably supported; (4) senatorial courtesy (closely linked to the consultative nominating process); (5) a nominee's perceived political unreliability on the part of the party in power; (6) the evident lack of qualification or limited ability of the nominee; (7) concerted, sustained opposition by interest or pressure groups; and (8) fear that the nominee would dramatically alter the Court's jurisprudential lineup. Usually several of these reasons—not one alone— figure in the rejection of a nominee, to which poor timing and poor presidential management of a nomination—e.g., Reagan in Bork's case—could readily be added.[204]

Another scholar, in analyzing the ill-fated nominations of Abe Fortas (1968), Clement F. Haynsworth Jr. (1969), G. Harrold Carswell (1970) and Robert H. Bork (1987), has focused on the "rich interplay among the three leading factors associated with unsuccessful Supreme Court nominations," specifically, "the Senate's perception of the nominee's ideology," the "timing of the nomination," and "a less appreciated" factor, "presidential management of the confirmation process."[205]

The timing of a nomination may create problems for confirmation of a Supreme Court nominee, especially against an election backdrop. Timing, for example, might be less favorable for a nomination if it is made during the last year of a President's term, if the President is not seeking re-election, if his re-election prospects are doubtful, or if an off-year election is approaching in which the President's party is expected to lose Senate seats. Such circum stances might influence some Senators to delay action on a nomination, in order to allow the next President to make the appointment or the next Senate to decide whether to confirm.[206]

Table 2. Supreme Court Nominations Not Confirmed by the Senate

Nominee	President	Date received in Senatea	Final action by Senate and/or Presidentb	Date(s) of Final Action
William Paterson	Washington	Feb. 27, 1793	Withdrawn	Feb. 28, 1793
John Rutledge (for Chief Justice)	Washington	Dec. 10, 1795	Rejected (10-14)	Dec. 15, 1795
Alexander Wolcott	Madison	Feb. 4, 1811	Rejected (9-24)	Feb. 13, 1811
John J. Crittenden	J.Q. Adams	Dec. 18, 1828	Postponed (23-17)	Feb. 12, 1829
Roger B. Taney	Jackson	Jan. 15, 1835	Postponed (24-21)	Mar. 3, 1835
John C. Spencer	Tyler	Jan. 9, 1844	Rejected (2 1-26)	Jan. 31, 1844
Reuben H. Walworth	Tyler	Mar. 13, 1844	Tabled (27-20), Withdrawn	June 15, 1844, June 17, 1844
Edward King	Tyler	June 5, 1844	Postponed (29-18)	June 15, 1844
John C. Spencer	Tyler	June 17, 1844	Withdrawn	June 17, 1844
Reuben H. Walworth	Tyler	June 17, 1844	No action recorded	
Reuben H. Walworth	Tyler	Dec. 10, 1844	Tabled, Withdrawn	Jan. 21, 1845, Feb. 6, 1845
Edward King	Tyler	Dec. 10, 1844	Tabled, Withdrawn	Jan. 21, 1845, Feb. 8, 1845
John M. Read	Tyler	Feb. 8, 1845	No action recorded	
George W. Woodward	Polk	Dec. 23, 1845	Rejected (20-29)	Jan. 22, 1846
Edward A. Bradford	Fillmore	Aug. 21, 1852	Tabled	Aug. 31, 1852
George E. Badger	Fillmore	Jan. 10, 1853	Postponed (26-25)	Feb. 11, 1853
William C. Micou	Fillmore	Feb. 24, 1853	No action recorded	
Jeremiah S. Black	Buchanan	Feb. 6, 1861	Motion to consider rejected (25-26)	Feb. 21, 1861

Table 2. (Continued)

Nominee	President	Date received in Senatea	Final action by Senate and/or Presidentb	Date(s) of Final Action
Henry Stanbery	A. Johnson	Apr. 16, 1866	No action recorded	
Ebenezer R. Hoar	Grant	Dec. 15, 1869	Rejected (24-33)	Feb. 3, 1870
George H. Williams (for Chief Justice)	Grant	Dec. 2, 1873	Withdrawn	Jan. 8, 1874
Caleb Cushing (for Chief Justice)	Grant	Jan. 9, 1874	Withdrawn	Jan. 14, 1874
Stanley Matthews	Hayes	Jan. 26, 1881	No action recorded	
Wm. B. Hornblower	Cleveland	Sep.19, 1893	No action recorded	
Wm. B. Hornblower	Cleveland	Dec. 6, 1893	Rejected (24-30)	Jan. 15, 1894
Wheeler H. Peckham	Cleveland	Jan. 22, 1894	Rejected (32-41)	Feb. 16, 1894
Pierce Butler	Harding	Nov. 23, 1922	No action recorded	
John. J. Parker	Hoover	Mar. 21, 1930	Rejected (39-41)	May 7, 1930
John M. Harlan	Eisenhower	Nov. 9, 1954	No action recorded	
Abe Fortas (for Chief Justice)	L. Johnson	June 26, 1968	Cloture motion defeated (45-43), Withdrawn	Oct. 1, 1968, Oct. 4, 1968
Homer Thornberry	L. Johnson	June 26, 1968	Withdrawn	Oct. 4, 1968
Clement F. Haynsworth Jr.	Nixon	Aug. 18, 1969	Rejected (45-55)	Nov. 21, 1969
G. Harrold Carswell	Nixon	Jan. 19, 1970	Rejected (45-51)	Apr. 8, 1970
Robert H. Bork	Reagan	July 7, 1987	Rejected (42-58)	Oct. 23, 1987
John G. Roberts Jr	Bush, G. W.	July 29, 2005	Withdrawn	Sep.6, 2005
Harriet E. Miers	Bush, G. W.	Oct. 7, 2005	Withdrawn	Oct. 28, 2005

Sources: *Journal of the Executive Proceedings of the Senate of the United States of America* (various volumes); CRS Report RL3 1171, *Supreme Court Nominations Not Confirmed*, 1789-2008, by Henry B. Hogue.

Notes: *Italics*—Later re-nominated and confirmed; **Boldface**—Later nominated for Chief Justice and confirmed.

a. The date in this column is the date on which the President's nomination message was received in the Senate. This date may differ from the date of the message itself.

b. Indicates whether there was final action by the Senate (rejecting, postponing action on, tabling, or rejecting a motion to close debate on the nomination) or by the President (withdrawing the nomination).

A nominee's prospects also may be put in jeopardy if a President has not used careful presidential management to pave the way for a smooth confirmation process. Among other things, sound presidential management of the process, it has been suggested, entails good-faith consultation with the

Senate before choosing a nominee, especially if the President's party is in the Senate minority. Another element of sound presidential management is selecting a nominee without obvious liabilities or attributes that are likely to generate serious Senate opposition.[207]

Calling upon the Judiciary Committee to Further Examine the Nomination

Sometimes, after a Supreme Court nomination has been reported, the Senate may delay considering or voting on the nomination, in order to have the Senate Judiciary Committee address new issues concerning the nominee or more fully examine issues that it addressed earlier. Opponents of a nomination may also seek such delay, through recommittal of the nomination to the committee, to defeat the nomination indirectly, by burying it in committee.

Recommittals of Supreme Court nominations

Although the Senate has never adopted a motion to reconsider a Supreme Court nomination after a confirmation vote, there have been at least eight pre-vote attempts to recommit Supreme Court nominations to the Judiciary Committee.[208] Only two of those were successful. In the first of these two instances, in 1873-1874, the nomination, after being recommitted, stalled in committee until it was withdrawn by the President. In the second instance, in 1925, the Judiciary Committee re-reported the nomination, which the Senate then confirmed.

On December 15, 1873, on the second day of its consideration of the nomination of attorney general George H. Williams to be Chief Justice, the Senate ordered the nomination to be recommitted to the Judiciary Committee.[209] The nomination had been favorably reported by the committee only four days earlier. During that four-day interval, however, various allegations were made against Williams, including charges that while attorney general he had used his office to influence decisions profiting private companies in which he held interests.[210] In ordering the nomination to be recommitted, the Senate authorized the Judiciary Committee "to send for persons and papers"[211]—in evident reference to the new allegations made against the nominee. Although the Judiciary Committee held hearings after the recommittal, it did not re-report the nomination back to the Senate. Amid press reports of significant opposition to the nomination both in the Judiciary

Committee and the Senate as a whole,[212] the nomination, at Williams's request, was withdrawn by President Ulysses S. Grant on January 8, 1874.[213]

On January 26, 1925, the Senate recommitted the Supreme Court nomination of Attorney General Harlan F. Stone to the Judiciary Committee. Earlier, on January 21, the Judiciary Committee had favorably reported the nomination to the Senate. However, one historian wrote, "Stone's unanimous Judiciary Committee approval ran into trouble when it reached the Senate floor."[214] A principal point of concern to some Senators was the decision made by Stone as attorney general in December 1924 to expand a federal criminal investigation of Senator Burton K. Wheeler (DMT)—an investigation initiated by Stone's predecessor as attorney general, Harry Daugherty. Stone's most prominent critic on this point, Montana's other Democratic Senator, Thomas J. Walsh, demanded that the nomination be returned to the Judiciary Committee.[215] By unanimous consent the Senate agreed, ordering the nomination to be "rereferred to the Committee on the Judiciary with a request that it be reported back to the Senate as soon as practicable."[216] Two days after the recommittal, on January 28, the Judiciary Committee held hearings, with the nominee, at the committee's invitation, taking the then-unprecedented step of appearing before the committee. Under lengthy cross examination by Senator Walsh and several other Senators, the nominee defended his role in the Wheeler investigation.[217] On February 2, 1925, the Judiciary Committee again reported the Stone nomination favorably to the Senate, "by voice vote, without dissent,"[218] and on February 5, 1925, the Senate confirmed Stone by a 71-6 vote.

Delay for additional committee hearings without recommitting the nomination

In 1991, during debate on Supreme Court nominee Clarence Thomas, the Senate—without recommitting the nomination to the Judiciary Committee—delayed its scheduled vote on the nomination specifically to allow the committee time for additional hearings on the nominee. On October 8, 1991, after four days of debate, the Senate, by unanimous consent, rescheduled its vote on the Thomas nomination, from October 8 to October 15. The purpose of this delay was to allow the Judiciary Committee to hold hearings on sexual harassment allegations made against the nominee by law professor Anita Hill, which had come to public light only after the Judiciary Committee had ordered the Thomas nomination to be reported, without recommendation, on September 27.[219] Following three days of hearings, on October 11, 12, and 13, 1991, at which the Judiciary Committee heard testimony from Judge Thomas,

Professor Hill, and other witnesses, the Senate, pursuant to its unanimous consent agreement, voted on the Thomas nomination as scheduled, on October 15, 1991, confirming the nominee by a 5 2-48 vote.

After Senate Confirmation

Under the Constitution, the Senate alone votes on whether to confirm presidential nominations, the House of Representatives having no formal involvement in the confirmation process. If the Senate votes to confirm the nomination, the secretary of the Senate then attests to a resolution of confirmation and transmits it to the White House.[220] In turn, the President signs a document, called a commission, officially appointing the individual to the Court. Next, the signed commission "is returned to the Justice Department for engraving the date of appointment (determined by the actual day the president signs the commission) and for the signature of the attorney general and the placing of the Justice Department seal."[221] The department then arranges for expedited delivery of the commission document to the new appointee.

Once the President has signed the commission, the incoming Justice may be sworn into office.[222] In fact, however, the new Justice actually takes two oaths of office—a judicial oath, as required by the Judiciary Act of 1789,[223] and a constitutional oath, which, as required by Article VI of the Constitution, is administered to Members of Congress and all executive and judicial officers. In recent years, the most common practice of new appointees has been to take their judicial oath in private, usually within the Court, and, as desired by the Presidents who nominated them, to take their constitutional oaths in nationally televised ceremonies at the White House.[224]

Subsequently, the Court itself, in its courtroom, also affords public recognition to the new Justice's appointment, in a formal ceremony called an "investiture," at which the Justice is sworn in yet again. This invitation-only event, for which reserved press seating is made available, is attended by the Court's other Justices, by family, friends, and former associates of the new Justice, and by outside dignitaries who may include the President and the attorney general.[225] The investiture typically occurs before the new Justice publicly takes his or her courtroom seat alongside the other members of the Court.[226]

CONCLUSION

Over the course of more than two centuries, the Supreme Court appointment process has undergone important changes, while remaining constant in other key respects. The process is now much longer than it used to be. From the appointment of the first Justices in 1789, continuing well into the 20th century, most Senate confirmations of Supreme Court nominees occurred within a week of the nominations being made by the President. In recent decades, by contrast, it has become the norm for appointment to the Court, from nomination by the President to confirmation by the Senate, to take from two to three months, with the process even longer if a nomination is controversial.

Prior to 1868, the Senate Judiciary Committee sometimes was excluded from, or played a perfunctory role in, the appointment process, but now the Judiciary Committee, rather than the Senate as a whole, invariably assumes the principal responsibility for investigating the background and qualifications of each Supreme Court nominee, and typically the committee conducts a close, intensive investigation of each nominee.

The process is also much more open now than it once was. From the outset, starting with George Washington, and for more than a hundred years thereafter, Presidents transmitted their nominations to the Senate without public fanfare, and the confirmation process that followed in the Senate Judiciary Committee and the Senate as a whole likewise occurred away from public view, in closed executive sessions. By contrast, in the modern appointment process, Presidents typically announce their Supreme Court nominations to the nation before broadcast television cameras in carefully staged presidential news events. In turn, nearly all of the official confirmation process that follows—confirmation hearings by the Judiciary Committee, the committee's vote on the nominee, Senate debate, and finally Senate vote on the nomination—is conducted in public session, receives intensive news media coverage, and is watched by hundreds of thousands (and sometimes millions) of American television viewers.

In another major change from earlier practice, there are now many more participants in the Supreme Court appointment process. Historically, nominees did not participate in the appointment process, but now they regularly appear before the Judiciary Committee. Likewise, in the modern era, public witnesses testify during each confirmation hearing. Among the witnesses are representatives of powerful interest groups, which often take positions in support of or in opposition to a nominee's confirmation. If a nominee is controversial, interest groups may commit themselves to sustained involvement in the confirmation process, mounting support for, or opposition to, a nominee at the very beginning of the process, and seeking through publicity, lobbying and grass-roots efforts of their members, to influence how both the Judiciary Committee and the Senate as a whole vote on the nomination.

From the beginning, an almost unchanging theme underlying the Supreme Court appointment process has been the assumed need for excellence or merit in a nominee as a requisite for appointment to the Court. The continuing expectation of high qualification in nominees has been demonstrated by the Senate's periodic rejection of nominees for alleged lack of qualification.

Also from the beginning, politics, as well as the search for excellence, has played a continuing, important role in Supreme Court appointments. The political nature of the Supreme Court appointment process becomes especially apparent when a President submits a nominee with controversial views, there are sharp partisan or ideological differences between the President and the Senate, or the outcome of important constitutional issues before the Court is seen to be at stake. Under these and other circumstances, divisions may occur in the Senate, bringing to the fore the differing political views of Senators supporting and those opposing the nominee.

If the nomination of a person to the Supreme Court sometimes produces confirmation battles, the appointment process at other times is remarkable for its lack of conflict, particularly when the Senate votes overwhelmingly for confirmation. Various factors might be present when a Supreme Court appointment process is characterized more by harmony than by conflict. At the start of the process, for example, there might be close consultation between the President and Senate Members over suitable candidates for the Court; the President may choose a distinguished, uncontroversial nominee who immediately attracts widespread support from Senators of both parties; the President's party might be in firm numerical superiority in the Senate (thus discouraging detractors of the nominee from mounting vigorous opposition); or a particular Court vacancy might not be regarded as of great moment to the future of the Court (in contrast to vacancy situations where opposing political interests perceive very much to be at stake).

Over more than two centuries, the Supreme Court appointment process has remained constant in one other, constitutionally fundamental respect—in the sharing of the appointment power between the President and the Senate. No Justice has ever been appointed for life to the Court except through this shared process of appointment (although, as noted earlier, Presidents on rare occasions have made temporary "recess appointments" to the Court without the Senate's consent).

Whenever a new Supreme Court vacancy occurs, the President and the Senate face a situation that is both unique and familiar. Unique are the political circumstances of the moment, and the legal controversies that loom before the Court at that point in time. Familiar are the basic roles to be performed in the appointment process. Following a pattern adhered to for more than 200 years, the President and the Senate will again share the appointment power. One will nominate, the other will decide whether to confirm. Only when the two reach agreement may a new Justice join eight others on the Supreme Court of the United States.

ADDITIONAL SOURCES

Abraham, Henry J. *Justices, Presidents, and Senators: A History of the U.S. Supreme Court Appointments from Washington to Clinton,* new and rev. ed. Lanham, MD: Rowman & Littlefield Publishers, Inc., 1999. 428 p.

——. *Justices and Presidents: A Political History of Appointments to the Supreme Court,* 3rd ed. New York: Oxford University Press, 1992. 467 p.

Atkinson, David N. *Leaving the Bench: Supreme Court Justices at the End.* Lawrence, KS: University Press of Kansas, 1999. 248 p.

Comiskey, Michael. *Seeking Justices: The Judging of Supreme Court Nominees.* Lawrence, KS: University Press of Kansas, 2004. 287 p.

Davis, Richard. *Electing Justice: Fixing the Supreme Court Nominating Process.* New York: Oxford University Press, 2005. 211 p.

Epstein, Lee, et al. *The Supreme Court Compendium: Data, Decisions & Developments,* 4th ed. Washington: Congressional Quarterly Inc., 2007. 808 p.

Gerhardt, Michael J. *The Federal Appointments Process.* Rev. ed. Durham, NC: Duke University Press, 2003. 406 p.

Geyh, Charles Cardner. *When Courts & Congress Collide: The Struggle for Control of America's Judicial System.* Ann Arbor, MI: University of Michigan Press, 2006. 332 p.

Greenburg, Jan Crawford. *The Inside Story of the Struggle for Control of the United States Supreme Court.* New York, Penguin Press, 2007. 340 p.

Harris, Joseph P. *The Advice and Consent of the Senate: A Study of the Confirmation of Appointments by the United States Senate.* Berkeley, CA:

University of California Press, 1953; reprint, New York: Greenwood Press, 1968. 457 p.

Jacobstein, J. Myron, and Roy M. Mersky. *The Rejected: Sketches of the 26 Men Nominated for the Supreme Court but Not Confirmed by the Senate.* Milpitas, CA: Toucan Valley Publications, 1993. 188 p.

Maltese, John Anthony. *The Selling of Supreme Court Nominees.* Baltimore: Johns Hopkins University Press, 1995. 193 p.

Massaro, John. *Supremely Political: The Role of Ideology and Presidential Management in Unsuccessful Supreme Court Nominations.* Albany, NY: State University of New York Press, 1990. 272 p.

Mersky, Roy M., and J. Myron Jacobstein, comp. *The Supreme Court of the United States:*

Hearings and Reports on Successful and Unsuccessful Nominations of Supreme Court Justices by the Senate Judiciary Committee, 1916-1994, 19 vols. Buffalo, NY: William S. Hein & Co., 1977-1996.

Nemacheck, Christine L. *Strategic Selection: Presidential Nomination of Supreme Court Justices from Herbert Hoover Through George W. Bush.* Charlottesville, VA: University of Virginia Press, 2007. 192 p.

Savage, David G. *Congressional Quarterly's Guide to the U.S. Supreme Court*, 4th ed., 2 vols. Washington: Congressional Quarterly Inc, 2004. 1272 p.

Silverstein, Mark. *Judicious Choices: The New Politics of Supreme Court Confirmations,* updated college ed. New York: W.W. Norton & Company, 1997. 192 p.

Ward, Artemus. *Deciding To Leave: The Politics of Retirement from the United States Supreme Court.* Albany, NY: State University of New York Press, 2003. 344 p.

Watson, George L, and John A. Stookey. *Shaping America: the Politics of Supreme Court Appointments.* New York: HarperCollins College Publishers, 1995. 259 p.

Wittes, Benjamin. *Confirmation Wars: Preserving Independent Courts in Angry Times.* Lanham, MD: Rowman & Littlefield Publishers, 2006. 168 p.

Wright, Benjamin Fletcher, ed. *The Federalist by Alexander Hamilton, James Madison, and John Jay.* Cambridge, MA: Belknap Press of Harvard University Press, 1966, pp. 480-484 (Federalist Paper 76—Hamilton, "The President and the Appointing Power"), pp. 489-496 (Federalist Paper 78—Hamilton, "The Judges as Guardians of the Constitution"), and pp. 497-499 (Federalist Paper 79—Hamilton, "The Position of the Judiciary").

Yalof, David Alistair *Pursuit of Justices: Presidential Politics and the Selection of Supreme Court Nominees*. Chicago, University of Chicago Press, 1999. 296 p.

End Notes

[1] U.S. Supreme Court, *The Supreme Court of the United States* (Washington: Published by the Supreme Court with the cooperation of the Supreme Court Historical Society, revised September 2006), p. 10. (Hereafter cited as Supreme Court, *Supreme Court of the United States.)*

[2] Of the 42 individuals who have served as President of the United States, six made only one Supreme Court nomination each, while three others were unable to make a single nomination to the Court since no vacancies occurred on the Court during their presidencies. See CRS Report RL3 3225, *Supreme Court Nominations, 1789-2006: Actions by the Senate, the Judiciary Committee, and the President*, by Denis Steven Rutkus and Maureen Bearden (under heading "Presidents Who Made the Nominations").

[3] For instance, nine vacancies occurred on the Court during a five-and-a-half year period of Franklin D. Roosevelt's presidency, with all of FDR's nine nominations to fill those vacancies confirmed by the Senate. The President with the largest number of Supreme Court confirmations in one term (apart from the first eight of George Washington's nominations—all in his first term, and all confirmed) was William Howard Taft, who, during his four years in office, made six Court nominations, all of which were confirmed by the Senate. Ibid.

[4] The annual terms of the Court, which by law begin on the first Monday of October, are usually concluded by late June of the following year.

[5] The Whte House, "The President's Remarks on Justice Souter," news release, May 1, 2009, at http://www.whitehouse.gov/blog/09/05/01/The-Presidents-Remarks-on-Justice-Souter/.

[6] U.S. Constitution, art. III, § 1.

[7] Alexander Hamilton, in Federalist Paper 78 ("The Judges as Guardians of the Constitution"), maintained that, while the judiciary was "in continual jeopardy of being overpowered, awed, or influenced by its coordinate branches ... , nothing can contribute so much to its firmness and independence as *permanency in office*." He added that if the courts "are to be considered as the bulwarks of a limited Constitution against legislative encroachments, this consideration will afford a strong argument for the *permanent tenure* of judicial offices, since *nothing will contribute so much as this to that independent spirit in the judges....*" (Emphases added.) Benjamin Fletcher Wright, ed., *The Federalist by Alexander Hamilton, James Madison, and John Jay* (Cambridge, MA: Belknap Press of Harvard University Press, 1966), p. 491 (first quote) and p. 494 (second quote). (Hereafter cited as Wright, *The Federalist.*)

[8] In 1804, the House of Representatives voted to impeach Justice Samuel Chase. The vote to impeach Chase, a staunch Federalist and outspoken critic of Jeffersonian Republican policies, was strictly along party lines. In 1805, after a Senate trial, Chase was acquitted after votes in the Senate fell short of the necessary two-thirds majority on any of the impeachment articles approved by the House. "Chase's impeachment and trial set a precedent of strict construction of the impeachment clause and bolstered the judiciary's claim of independence from political tampering." David G. Savage, *Guide to the U.S. Supreme Court*, 4th ed. (Washington: Congressional Quarterly Inc., 2004), vol. 1, p. 258. (Hereafter cited as Savage, *Guide to the U.S. Supreme Court.*)

[9] A Supreme Court booklet notes that since the formation of the Court in 1790, there have been only 17 Chief Justices and 98 Associate Justices, "with Justices serving for an average of 15 years." Supreme Court, *Supreme Court of the United States,* p. 10.

[10] The decision of the Framers at the Constitutional Convention of 1787 to have the President and the Senate share in the appointment of the Supreme Court Justices and other principal officers of the government, one scholar wrote, was a compromise reached between "one group of men [who] feared the abuse of the appointing power by the executive and favored appointments by the legislative body," and "another group of more resolute men, eager to establish a strong national government with a vigorous administration, [who] favored the granting of the power of appointment to the President." Joseph P. Harris, *The Advice and Consent of the Senate: A Study of the Confirmation of Appointments by the United States Senate* (Berkeley, CA: University of California Press, 1953; reprint, New York: Greenwood Press, 1968), p. 33. (Hereafter cited as Harris, *Advice and Consent of the Senate.*)

[11] Consider, for example, President John Adams's fateful nomination in 1801 of John Marshall. During his more than 34 years of service as Chief Justice, Marshall, "more than any other individual in the history of the Court, determined the developing character of America's Federal constitutional system" and "raised the Court from its lowly, if not discredited, position to a level of equality with the executive and legislative branches." Henry J. Abraham, *Justices and Presidents: A Political History of Appointments to the Supreme Court,* 3rd ed. (New York: Oxford University Press, 1992), p. 83. (Hereafter cited as Abraham, *Justices and Presidents.*) Looking back on his appointment a quarter century before, Adams in 1826 was quoted as saying, "My gift of John Marshall to the people of the United States was the proudest act of my life." Charles Warren, *The Supreme Court in United States History*, rev. edition, 2 vols. (Boston: Little Brown, 1926), vol. 1, p. 178.

[12] "By well-established custom, the Senate accords the President wide latitude in the selection of the members of his Cabinet, who are regarded as his chief assistants and advisers. It is recognized that unless he is given a free hand in the choice of his Cabinet, he cannot be held responsible for the administration of the executive branch." Harris, *Advice and Consent of the Senate*, p. 259.

[13] The Senate "is perhaps most acutely attentive to its [advise and consent] duty when it considers a nominee to the Supreme Court. That this is so reflects not only the importance of our Nation's highest tribunal, but also our recognition that while Members of the Congress and Presidents come and go ..., the tenure of a Supreme Court Justice can span generations." Sen. Daniel P. Moynihan, debate in Senate on Supreme Court nomination of Ruth Bader Ginsburg, *Congressional Record*, vol. 139, August 2, 1993, p. 18142.

[14] See CRS Report RL3 3225, *Supreme Court Nominations, 1789 - 2006: Actions by the Senate, the Judiciary Committee, and the President*, the table at the end of the report, which lists all 158 Supreme Court nominations since 1789. The table shows that a lesser number of individuals, 139, were actually nominated to the Court, with some of them nominated more than once. The table includes the names of eight nominees who, subsequent to Senate confirmation, did not assume the office to which they had been appointed (with seven having declined the office, and one having died before assuming it).

[15] The first rejection by the Senate of a Supreme Court nominee occurred on December 15, 1795, when the Senate voted 14 to 10 not to confirm President George Washington's nomination of John Rutledge of South Carolina to be Chief Justice. See **Table 2** in the following pages of this report, listing all 36 Supreme Court nominations not confirmed by the Senate. Besides listing the unconfirmed nominations of persons nominated only once to the Court, the table includes the unconfirmed nominations of persons who were (1) nominated more than once and never confirmed; (2) re-nominated to the same Court position and then confirmed; or (3) nominated unsuccessfully for Associate Justice, only to be re-nominated for Chief Justice and then confirmed. For more complete information about the 36 Supreme Court nominations not confirmed by the Senate, including, most recently, the withdrawn nomination of Harriet E. Miers in 2005, see CRS Report RL3 1171, *Supreme Court*

Nominations Not Confirmed, 1789-2008, by Henry B. Hogue. For short narratives regarding the Rutledge confirmation defeat and 25 subsequent Supreme Court nominees who failed to gain Senate confirmation, see J. Myron Jacobstein and Roy M. Mersky, *The Rejected* (Milpitas, CA: Toucan Valley Publications, 1993). (Hereafter cited as Jacobstein and Mersky, *The Rejected*.) Since it was published in 1993, *The Rejected* lacks a narrative for the failed Miers nomination. For such an account on the Miers nomination, see Jan Crawford Greenburg, *Supreme Conflict: The Inside Story of the Struggle for Control of the United States Supreme Court* (New York: Penguin Press, 2007), pp. 245-284. (Hereafter cited as Greenburg, *Supreme Conflict*.)

[16] The first Supreme Court nominee to be re-nominated and confirmed after his first nomination failed to be confirmed was William Paterson of New Jersey in 1793. Paterson was first nominated on February 27, 1793, by President George Washington. The President, however, withdrew the nomination a day later, citing a constitutional technicality. In his withdrawal message (U.S. Congress, Senate, *Journal of the Executive Proceedings of the Senate of the United States of America*, vol. 1, p. 135), President Washington indicated that the nomination was in violation of Article I, Section 6 of the Constitution, which provides: "No Senator or Representative shall, during the Time for which he was elected, be appointed to any civil Office ..., which shall have been created ... during such time ...." Paterson had been a member of the Senate when the Judiciary Act of 1789 was passed, creating the Associate Justice position to which Washington nominated Paterson in February 1793. Though Paterson had resigned from the Senate in 1790, the Senate term to which he had been elected would not conclude until March 3, 1793. Washington re-nominated Paterson on March 4, 1793, and later that day a special session of the Senate of a new Congress confirmed the nominee by voice vote.

Another Court nominee to be re-nominated and then confirmed was Pierce Butler of Minnesota in 1922. Butler was first nominated by President Warren G. Harding on November 23, 1922, during the 3rd session of the 67th Congress. Although reported favorably by the Judiciary Committee, the nomination failed to be confirmed before the end of the 3rd session. President Harding re-nominated Butler on December 5, 1922, during the 4th session of the 67th Congress, and shortly thereafter, on December 22, 1922, the Senate confirmed Butler by a 61-8 roll-call vote.

A third Court nominee to be re-nominated and then confirmed was John M. Harlan II of New York. Harlan was first nominated by President Dwight D. Eisenhower on November 9, 1954, but the nomination received no action in the Senate before the final adjournment of the 83rd Congress less than a month later. President Eisenhower re-nominated Harlan on January 10, 1955, at the beginning of the 84th Congress, and shortly thereafter, on March 16, 1955, the Senate confirmed Harlan by a 71-11 roll-call vote.

Two other nominees who were not confirmed the first time only to be later re-nominated and confirmed received Senate confirmation in spite of significant Senate opposition. One was Roger B. Taney, nominated twice by President Andrew Jackson in 1835, and Stanley Matthews, nominated first by President Rutherford B. Hayes in 1881 and by President James A. Garfield, later in 1881. Taney's first nomination, to Associate Justice, was postponed indefinitely by the Senate. During the next Congress, he was re-nominated and confirmed as Chief Justice by a 29-15 roll-call vote in the Senate. Mathews' first nomination was never reported out of committee, but in the following Congress, under a new President, he was re-nominated and confirmed by a 24-23 roll-call vote.

The final nominee not confirmed but later re-nominated and confirmed was current Chief Justice John G. Roberts. As noted previously in this report, Judge Roberts was first nominated to replace Associate Justice Sandra Day O'Connor, but when Chief Justice Rehnquist died suddenly, President Bush withdrew his nomination and resubmitted it for the position of Chief Justice.

[17] During the 1967-2006 period, two other Court nominations—the Associate Justice nominations in 2005 of John G. Roberts Jr. and Harriet E. Miers—were withdrawn by the

President before receiving hearings. On the day his nomination was withdrawn, however, Judge Roberts was re-nominated to be Chief Justice and, 39 days later, confirmed.

[18] According to one author, when Justice Sandra Day O'Connor in 2005 announced her plan to retire, the Court was regarded as playing an extremely important role in American life. "For the past fifty years, beginning under the leadership of Earl Warren, the Court had confronted America's most pressing social controversies. The Court showed little hesitation in interjecting itself into those disputes and attempting to solve the nation's most vexing problems from the bench, even if that meant wresting them away from the state legislatures and the Congress." In the process, the Court "became a moral compass," identifying "new constitutional rights" not specifically addressed in the Constitution. "Liberals believed that was an entirely proper role for the court, especially since the other branches of government had failed so miserably in the area of civil rights." By contrast, conservatives "saw a Supreme Court that had arrogantly grabbed power for itself." Greenburg, *Supreme Conflict*, pp. 23-24.

[19] As noted above, a Supreme Court vacancy also would occur if a Justice were removed by Congress through the impeachment process, but no Justice has ever been removed from the Court in this way. For a comprehensive review of how and why past Supreme Court Justices have left the Court, see Artemus Ward, *Deciding To Leave: The Politics of Retirement from the United States Supreme Court* (Albany, NY: State University of New York Press, 2003), pp. 25-223. Ward, in introduction at p. 7, explained that his book, among other things, examines the extent to which Justices, in their retirement decisions, have been "motivated by strategic, partisan, personal, and institutional concerns."

[20] For a book-length examination of how Presidents since World War II have selected nominees to serve on the Supreme Court, see David Alistair Yalof, *Pursuit of Justices: Presidential Politics and the Selection of Supreme Court Nominees* (Chicago: University of Chicago Press, 1999). (Hereafter cited as Yalof, *Pursuit of Justices*.) See also Greenburg, *Supreme Conflict*, which examined in depth the processes followed by the Administrations of Presidents Ronald Reagan, George H. W. Bush, William J. Clinton, and George W. Bush in selecting Supreme Court nominees; and Christine L. Nemacheck, *Strategic Selection: Presidential Nomination of Supreme Court Justices from Herbert Hoover Through George W. Bush* (Charlottesville, VA: University of Virginia Press, 2007).

[21] See, for example, John Ferling, "The Senate and Federal Judges: The Intent of the Founding Fathers," *Capitol Studies*, vol. 2, Winter 1974, p. 66: "Since the convention acted at a time when nearly every state constitution, and the Articles of Confederation, permitted a legislative voice in the selection of judges, it is inconceivable that the delegates could have intended something less than full Senate participation in the appointment process."

[22] See, for example, Harris, *Advice and Consent of the Senate*, p. 34: "The debates in the Convention do not support the thesis since advanced that the framers of the Constitution intended that the President should secure the advice—that is, the recommendations—of the Senate or of individual members, before making a nomination."

[23] Michael J. Gerhardt, *The Federal Appointments Process* (Durham, NC: Duke University Press, 2000), p. 33. (Hereafter cited as Gerhardt, *The Federal Appointment Process.*) The Constitution, Gerhardt added, "does not mandate any formal prenomination role for the Senate to consult with the president; nor does it impose any obligation on the president to consult with the Senate prior to nominating people to confirmable posts. The Constitution does, however, make it clear that the president or his nominees may have to pay a price if he ignores the Senate's advice." Ibid.

[24] "To a certain extent, presidents have always looked to the Senate for recommendations and subsequently relied on a nominee's backers there to help move the nomination through the Senate." George L. Watson and John A. Stookey, *Shaping America: The Politics of Supreme Court Appointments* (New York, HarperCollins College Publishers, 1995), p. 78. (Hereafter cited as Watson and Stookey, *Shaping America*.)

[25] President Clinton's search for a successor to retiring Justice Harry A. Blackmun, during the spring of 1994, is illustrative of a President seeking and receiving Senate advice. According to one report, the President, as he came close to a decision after holding his options "close to the vest" for more than a month, "began for the first time to consult with leading senators about his top candidates for the Court seat and solicited advice about prospects for easy confirmation." The advice he received included "sharp Republican opposition to one of his leading choices, Interior Secretary Bruce Babbitt." Gwen Ifill, "Clinton Again Puts Off Decision on Nominee for Court," *The New York Times*, May 11, 1994, p. A16.
In 2005, the Administration of President George W. Bush took pains to engage in a level of consultation with Senators over prospective Supreme Court nominations that White House officials called unprecedented. Prior to the President's nominations to the Court of John G. Roberts Jr., Harriet E. Miers, and Samuel A. Alito Jr., the President and his aides reportedly consulted with, and sought input from, the vast majority of the Senate's Members. Prior to announcing the Miers nomination, for instance, it was reported that "the President and his staff talked with more than 80 Senators," although "some Democrats questioned whether the process was just for show." Deb Riechmann, "Bush Expected to Name High Court Nominee," Associated Press Online, September 30, 2005 (accessed at http://www.nexis.com). According to a White House spokesman, the more than 80 Senators included all 18 members of the Senate Judiciary Committee and over two-thirds of Senate Democrats. Steve Holland, "Bush Completes Consultations, Nears Court Decision," Reuters News, September 30, 2005 (accessed at http://global.factiva.com).

[26] "Numerous instances of the application of senatorial courtesy are on record, with the practice at least partially accounting for rejection of several nominations to the Supreme Court." Henry J. Abraham, *Justices, Presidents and Senators: A History of the U.S. Supreme Court Appointments from Washington to Clinton*, new and rev. ed. (New York: Rowman & Littlefield Publishers, 1999), pp. 19-20. (Hereafter cited as Abraham, *Justices, Presidents and Senators.*) Senatorial courtesy, Abraham wrote, appeared to have been the sole factor in President Grover Cleveland's unsuccessful nominations of William B. Hornblower (1893) and Wheeler H. Peckham (1894), both of New York. Each was rejected by the Senate after Senator David B. Hill (D-NY) invoked senatorial courtesy.

[27] In 1987, for instance, some Senators publicly warned President Reagan that he could expect problems in the Senate if he nominated U.S. appellate court judge Robert H. Bork to replace vacating Justice Lewis F. Powell. Among them, Sen. Robert C. Byrd (D-WV) said the Reagan Administration would be "inviting problems" by nominating Bork. The chair of the Senate Judiciary Committee, Joseph R. Biden Jr. (D-DE), said that, while Bork was a "brilliant man," it did "not mean that there should be six or seven or eight or even five Borks" on the Court. Helen Dewar and Howard Kurtz, "Byrd Threatens Stall on Court Confirmation," *The Washington Post*, June 30, 1987, p. A7. In what was regarded as a thinly veiled reference to a possible Bork nomination, Senate Majority Whip Alan Cranston (D-CA) called on Senate Democrats to form a "solid phalanx" to block an "ideological court coup" by President Reagan. Al Kamen and Ruth Marcus, "Nomination to Test Senate Role in Shaping of Supreme Court," *The Washington Post*, July 1, 1987, p. A9. President Reagan, nonetheless, nominated Judge Bork, only to have the nomination meet widespread Senate opposition and ultimate Senate rejection.

[28] Modern Presidents, one scholar wrote, "are often forced to arbitrate among factions within their own administrations, each pursuing its own interests and agendas." In recent Administrations, he maintained, the final choice of a nominee "has usually reflected one advisor's hard-won victory over his rivals, without necessarily accounting for the president's other political interests." Yalof, *Pursuit of Justices*, p. 3.

[29] For numerous examples of Justices advising Presidents regarding Supreme Court appointments, both in the 19th and 20th centuries, see Abraham, *Justices, Presidents and Senators*, pp. 2 1-23; see also in Abraham's earlier work, *Justices and Presidents*, pp. 186-187 (Chief Justice William Howard Taft's influence over President Warren G. Harding); pp.

233-234 (Justice Felix Frankfurter's advice to President Franklin D. Roosevelt); p. 243 (former Chief Justice Charles Evans Hughes's and former Justice Owen J. Roberts's advice to President Harry S Truman); and pp. 305-306 (Chief Justice Warren Burger's advice to President Richard M. Nixon).

[30] Watson and Stookey, *Shaping America*, pp. 5 8-59.

[31] Considerations of geographic representation, for example, influenced President George Washington in 1789, to divide his first six appointments to the Court between three nominees from the North and three from the South. See Watson and Stookey, *Shaping America*, p. 60, and Abraham, *Justices, Presidents, and Senators*, pp. 59-60. President Reagan in 1981, for example, was sensitive to the absence of any female Justices on the Court. In announcing his choice of Sandra Day O'Connor to replace vacating Justice Potter Stewart, President Reagan noted that "during my campaign for the Presidency, I made a commitment that one of my first appointments to the Supreme Court vacancy would be the most qualified woman that I could possibly find." U.S. President (Reagan), "Remarks Announcing the Intention To Nominate Sandra Day O'Connor To Be an Associate Justice of the Supreme Court of the United States, July 7, 1981," *Public Papers of the Presidents of the United States, Ronald Reagan, 1981* (Washington: GPO, 1982), p. 596

[32] While the "desire to appoint justices sympathetic to their own ideological and policy views may drive most presidents in selecting judges," the field of potentially acceptable nominees for most presidents, according to Watson and Stookey, is narrowed down by at least five "subsidiary motivations"—(1) rewarding personal or political support, (2) representing certain interests, (3) cultivating political support, (4) ensuring a safe nominee, and 5) picking the most qualified nominee. Watson and Stookey, *Shaping America*, p. 59.

[33] Commenting on the nature of the Court's work, and the degree of qualification required of those who serve on the Court, the American Bar Association, in a recently published booklet, said the following: "The significance, range and complexity of the issues considered by the justices, as well as the finality and nation-wide impact of the Supreme Court's decisions, are among the factors that require the appointment of a nominee of exceptional ability." American Bar Association, *ABA Standing Committee on the Federal Judiciary: What It Is and How it Works*, pp. 9-10 (accessed April 26, 2007, at http://www.abanet.org/scfedjud/).

[34] One of the "unwritten codes," two scholars on the judiciary have written, "is that a judicial appointment is different from run-of-the-mill patronage. Thus, although the political rules may allow a president to reward an old ally with a seat on the bench, even here tradition has created an expectation that the would-be judge have some reputation for professional competence, the more so as the judgeship in question goes from the trial court to the appeals court to the Supreme Court level." Robert A. Carp and Ronald A. Stidham, *Judicial Process in America*, 3rd ed. (Washington: CQ Press, 1996), pp. 240-241.

[35] President Gerald R. Ford, for example, said he believed his nominee, U.S. appellate court judge John Paul Stevens, "to be best qualified to serve as an Associate Justice of the Supreme Court." U.S. President (Ford), "Remarks Announcing Intention To Nominate John Paul Stevens To Be an Associate Justice of the Supreme Court, November 28, 1975," *Public Papers of the Presidents of the United States, Gerald R. Ford, 1975*, Book II (Washington: GPO, 1977), p. 1917. Similarly, in 1991, President George H. W. Bush said of nominee Clarence Thomas, "I believe he'll be a great justice. He is the best person for this position." U.S. President (Bush, George H.W.), "The President's News Conference in Kennebunkport, Maine, July 1, 1991," *Public Papers of the President of the United States, George Bush,1991*, Book II (Washington: GPO, 1992), p. 801. More recently, in 2005, President George W. Bush, in announcing his nomination of John G. Roberts Jr. to be an Associate Justice, described his nominee as having "superb credentials"; as serving "on one of the most influential courts in the Nation"; and as known, prior to becoming a judge, "as one of the most distinguished and talented attorneys in America." U.S. President (Bush, George W.), "Address to the Nation Announcing the Nomination of John G. Roberts, Jr. To

Be an Associate Justice of the United States Supreme Court," *Weekly Compilation of Presidential* Documents, vol. 41, July 25, 2005, p. 1192.

[36] For lists of the professional, educational, and political backgrounds of every Justice who has served on the Court, see Lee Epstein et al., *The Supreme Court Compendium: Data, Decisions & Developments*, 4th ed. (Washington: Congressional Quarterly Inc., 2007), pp. 291-341. (Hereafter cited as Epstein, *Supreme Court Compendium.*)

[37] A legal scholar notes that while the Constitution "does not preclude a president from nominating nonlawyers to key Justice Department posts or federal judgeships," the delegates to the constitutional convention and the ratifiers "did occasionally express their expectation that a president would nominate qualified people to federal judgeships and other important governmental offices; but those comments were expressions of hope and concern about the consequences of and the need to devise a check against a president's failure to nominate qualified people, particularly in the absence of any constitutionally required minimal criteria for certain positions." Gerhardt, *The Federal Appointments Process*, p. 35.

[38] Watson and Stookey, *Shaping America*, p. 64.

[39] In Federalist Paper 78 ("Judges as Guardians of the Constitution"), Hamilton extolled the "benefits of the integrity and moderation of the Judiciary," which, he said, commanded "the esteem and applause of all the virtuous and disinterested." Further, he maintained, there could "be but few men" in society who would "unite the requisite integrity with the requisite knowledge" to "qualify them for the stations of judges." Wright, *The Federalist*, p. 495 (first quote) and p. 496 (second quote).

[40] Miller Center of Public Affairs, *Improving the Process of Appointing Federal Judges: A Report of the Miller Center Commission on the Selection of Federal Judges* (Charlottesville, VA: University of Virginia, May 1996), p. 10.

[41] For example, President George H.W. Bush, in announcing the nomination of David H. Souter to be an Associate Justice in 1990, declared that he wanted "a Justice who will ably and fairly interpret the law," and then added, "I believe that we've set a good example of selecting a fair arbiter of the law." U.S. President (Bush, George H.W.), "Remarks Announcing the Nomination of David H. Souter To Be an Associate Justice of the Supreme Court of the United States and a Question-and-Answer Session with Reporters," *Public Papers of the President of the United States*, *George Bush, 1990*, Book II (Washington: GPO, 1991), p. 1047. Most recently, in 2005, in announcing the nomination of Samuel A. Alito Jr. to be an Associate Justice, President George W. Bush said he was confident that the Senate would be impressed not only by Judge Alito's "distinguished record" but also by his "measured judicial temperament and his tremendous personal integrity." U.S. President (Bush, George W.), "Remarks Announcing the Nomination of Samuel A. Alito Jr., To Be an Associate Justice of the United States Supreme Court," *Weekly Compilation of Presidential Documents,* vol. 41, November 7, 2005, p. 1626.

[42] See CRS Report RL32821, *The Chief Justice of the United States: Responsibilities of the Office and Process for Appointment*, by Denis Steven Rutkus and Lorraine H. Tong (under heading "Criteria for Selecting a Nominee"). (See also Greenburg, *Supreme Conflict*, pp. 23 8-243 (discussing the assessment of the Administration of President George W. Bush in 2005 that John G. Roberts's leadership abilities and interpersonal skills were important qualities needed in a person under consideration for appointment to be Chief Justice).

[43] Perhaps the most extensive use of private attorneys for this purpose was made by President Clinton in the spring of 1993 during his consideration of candidates to fill the Supreme Court seat of retiring Justice Byron White. President Clinton, it was reported, utilized a team of 75 lawyers in the Washington, DC, area, who "pore[d] over briefs," analyzed "mountains of opinions and speeches" and "comb[ed] through financial records," of the "final contenders" for the Court appointment—from whom the President ultimately selected U.S. appellate court judge Ruth Bader Ginsburg. The team funneled their analyses to the White House counsel, "who, along with other aides, advised the president during the search for a justice." Under the team's ground rules, its work was performed on a confidential

basis, with contact between its lawyers and White House aides prohibited. Private attorneys were relied on in this way at least partly because, at that early point in the Clinton presidency, a judicial search team for the Administration was not yet in place in the Department of Justice. Daniel Klaidman, "Who Are Clinton's Vetters, and Why the Big Secret?" *Legal Times*, vol. 16, June 21, 1993, pp. 1, 22-23.

44 "During President Gerald R. Ford's search to fill a high court vacancy, Attorney General Edward Levi discreetly asked a small group of distinguished constitutional scholars to review opinions and other legal writings of a number of candidates." Ibid. (Klaidman), p. 23.

45 From the early 1950s through the 1990s, the ABA's Standing Committee on the Federal Judiciary played a quasi-official evaluating role to every President regarding the qualifications of prospective nominees to the lower federal courts (providing its evaluations of judicial candidates to the White House via the Department of Justice). Three Presidents, each on at least one occasion, submitted to the ABA committee the names of prospective Supreme Court candidates as well (Dwight D. Eisenhower in 1957, Richard M. Nixon in 1971, and Gerald R. Ford in 1975). The committee, however, was unsuccessful in efforts to secure from Presidents a permanent role in evaluating potential Supreme Court nominees. See generally CRS Report 96-446, *The American Bar Association's Standing Committee on Federal Judiciary: A Historical Overview*, by Denis Steven Rutkus (available from author; hereafter cited as CRS Report 96-446, *ABA Historical Overview*), for a narrative tracing the evolution of the ABA committee's role from the 1940s to 1995, and specifically pp. 8-9, 31-32, and 35 regarding its role in advising Eisenhower, Nixon, and Ford, respectively. See also Amy Goldstein, "Bush Curtails ABA Role in Selecting U.S. Judges," *The Washington Post*, March 23, 2001, pp. A1, A12, regarding the decision of President George W. Bush to discontinue the ABA committee's longstanding role in pre-nomination evaluations of lower court candidates.

46 The four most recent Presidents—Reagan, George H.W. Bush, Clinton, and George W. Bush—all personally interviewed their final candidates before selecting a nominee. "Both Reagan and the elder Bush relied more on their staffs to pare down the list of nominees. They interviewed one or, at most, two prospects before making their decision, compared to the five George W. Bush interviewed to replace Sandra Day O'Connor." Greenburg, *Supreme Conflict*, p. 314.

47 Greenburg, *Supreme Conflict*, p. 241.

48 Presidents Reagan and George H. W. Bush, for instance, selected most of their Supreme Court nominees quickly, within days of the vacating Justices announcing their retirements from the Court. President Clinton, however, took more time in selecting his two Supreme Court nominees, nominating Ruth Bader Ginsburg on June 22, 1993, three months after the retirement announcement of Justice Byron R. White, and nominating Stephen G. Breyer on May 17, 1994, five weeks after the retirement announcement of Justice Harry A. Blackmun. Likewise, President George W. Bush's first two Supreme Court selections were not made immediately upon the heels of a Justice's retirement announcement: President Bush announced his choice of John G. Roberts Jr. to succeed Sandra Day O'Connor 18 days after she submitted her retirement letter to the President, and he announced his choice of Harriet E. Miers to succeed Justice O'Connor 28 days after withdrawing the aforementioned Roberts nomination. By contrast, President Bush moved much more swiftly in selecting a nominee to succeed Chief Justice William H. Rehnquist, announcing his choice of John G. Roberts Jr. for that office two days after the death of Chief Justice Rehnquist on September 3, 2005. Likewise, he moved swiftly in selecting a third nominee to succeed Justice O'Connor, announcing his choice of Samuel A. Alito Jr. for that office on October 31, 2005, four days after the Miers nomination to that office was withdrawn. For more detailed information about how quickly 20th century Presidents and President George W. Bush selected Supreme Court nominees, see Tables 1 and 2 in CRS Report RL33 118, *Speed of*

Presidential and Senate Actions on Supreme Court Nominations, 1900-2006, by R. Sam Garrett, Denis Steven Rutkus, and Curtis W. Copeland.

[49] It is "precisely when presidents fail to require thorough checks," two scholars have written, "that trouble is likely." As illustrative, they cite the FBI investigation of President Richard M. Nixon's Supreme Court nominee Clement F. Haynsworth Jr. in 1969. "Unfortunately for both Haynsworth and the president, the cursory FBI check left unrevealed questions of financial dealings and conflicts of interest that would eventually doom the nomination. Without learning from the first mistake, the Nixon Administration rushed headlong into another hurried selection, Harrold Carswell, without full knowledge of flaws that would prove fatal in his background. A similar failure occurred as the Reagan Administration rushed to bring forth a nominee in the wake of the Bork defeat. In this instance, the rushed investigation failed to uncover the marijuana episodes of Douglas Ginsburg, which led to another presidential setback in the appointment process." Watson and Stookey, *Shaping America*, p. 82.

[50] Days after Justice White's retirement announcement on March 19, 1993, one newspaper reported that, while President Clinton had "an interest in a swift nomination so he can move on to other priorities, White's early notice gives him weeks, even months, to complete the selection process." Joan Biskupic, "Promises, Pressure in Court Search," *The Washington Post*, March 21, 1993, p. A1. The President ultimately nominated a successor to Justice White, U.S. appellate court judge Ruth Bader Ginsburg, on June 22, 1993, and the Senate confirmed that nomination on August 3, 1993.

[51] Justice Blackmun reportedly had given even more advance notice to the President, having privately informed him, on or about January 1, 1994, of his intention to retire before the start of the next Court term in October 1994. See Douglas Jehl, "Mitchell Viewed as Top Candidate for High Court," *The New York Times,* April 7, 1994, p. A1; Tony Mauro, "How Blackmun Hid Retirement Plans," *New Jersey Law Journal*, April 25, 1994, p. 18 (accessed at http://www.nexis.com). Later, on the eve of his public retirement announcement, on April 6, 1994, Justice Blackmun was reported to have told friends "he wanted to make sure there would be ample time for a successor to be confirmed by the Senate and prepare for the start of a new term in October." Ruth Marcus, "Blackmun Set To Leave High Court, *The Washington Post*, April 6, 1994, p. A1. Despite the long lead time afforded by Justice Blackmun's announcement, White House advisers reportedly believed it was "important to act quickly" to name a successor to Blackmun, in order to "avoid a repeat of last year's drawn out process" in which President Clinton engaged in a "very public, three-month search" before nominating Ruth Bader Ginsburg to the Court. Ibid., pp. A1, A7. After Justice Blackmun's announcement, President Clinton deliberated five weeks before announcing, on May 13, 1994, his selection of U.S. appellate court judge Stephen G. Breyer to be his Supreme Court nominee.

[52] Sandra Day O'Connor, letter to President George W. Bush, July 1, 2005 (accessed at http://www.supremecourtus.gov/).

[53] U.S. President (Bush, George W.), "Resignation of Justice Sandra Day O'Connor from the Supreme Court of the United States," Weekly Compilation of Presidential Documents, vol. 41, July 4, 2005, p. 1108.

[54] While President Bush announced his selection of Roberts to be an Associate Justice nominee on July 19, 2005, he formally transmitted his nomination of Roberts to the Senate 10 days later.

[55] Specifically, Article II, Section 2, Clause 3 of the U.S. Constitution empowers the President "to fill up all Vacancies that may happen during the Recess of the Senate, by granting Commissions which shall expire at the End of their next Session."

[56] For a list and discussion of the 12 recess appointments to the Court, see Henry B. Hogue, "The Law: Recess Appointments to Article III Courts," *Presidential Studies Quarterly*, vol. 34, September 2004, pp. 656-673. For more information on judicial recess appointments, see

CRS Report RL3 3009, *Recess Appointments: A Legal Overview*, by T. J. Halstead, and CRS Report RS22039, *Federal Recess Judges*, by Louis Fisher (available from author).

57 Adopted by the Senate on August 29, 1960, by a 48-3 7 vote, S.Res. 334 expressed the sense of the Senate that recess appointments to the Supreme Court "should not be made, except under unusual circumstances and for the purpose of preventing or ending a demonstrable breakdown in the administration of the Court's business." Proponents of the resolution contended, among other things, that judicial independence would be affected if Supreme Court recess appointees, during the probationary period of their appointment, took positions to please the President (in order not to have the President withdraw their nominations) or to please the Senate (in order to gain confirmation of their nominations). It also was argued that Senate investigation of nominations of these recess appointees was made difficult by the oath preventing sitting Justices from testifying about matters pending before the Court. Opponents, however, said, among other things, that the resolution was an attempt to restrict the President's constitutional recess appointment powers and that recess appointments were sometimes called for in order to keep the Court at full strength and to prevent evenly split rulings by its members. "Opposition to Recess Appointments to the Supreme Court," debate in Senate on S.Res. 334, *Congressional Record*, vol. 106, August 29, 1960, pp. 18130-18145. See also CRS Report RL3 1112, *Recess Appointments of Federal Judges*, by Louis Fisher, pp. 16-18 (available from author).

58 U.S. v. Woodley, 751 F.2d 1008 (9th Cir. 1985), *cert. denied*, 475 U.S. 1049 (1986).

59 Evans v. Stephens, 387 F.3d 1220 (1 1th Cir. 2004), *cert. denied*, 544 U.S. 942 (2005).

60 A notable, relatively recent instance in which the possibility of a recess appointment to the Court was raised occurred on July 28, 1987, when Senate Minority Leader Robert Dole (R-KS) observed that President Reagan had the constitutional prerogative to recess appoint U.S. appellate court judge Robert H. Bork to the Court. Earlier that month Judge Bork had been nominated to the Court, and, at the time of Senator Dole's statement, the chair of Senate Judiciary Committee, Sen. Joseph R. Biden Jr. (D-DE), had scheduled confirmation hearings to begin on September 15. With various Republican Senators accusing Senate Democrats of delaying the Bork hearings, Senator Dole offered as "food for thought" the possibility of President Reagan making a recess appointment of Judge Bork during Congress's August recess. Michael Fumento, "Reagan Has Power To Seat Bork While Senate Stalls: Dole," *The Washington Times*, July 28, 1987, p. A3; also, Edward Walsh, "Reagan's Power To Make Recess Appointment Is Noted," *The Washington Post*, July 28, 1987, p. A8. Judge Bork, however, did not receive a recess appointment and, as a Supreme Court nominee, was rejected by the Senate in a 58-42 vote on October 23, 1987.

61 As explained earlier, Article II, Section 2, Clause 2, in pertinent part, provides simply that the President "shall nominate, and by and with the Advice and Consent of the Senate, shall appoint ... Judges of the supreme Court."

62 U.S. Congress, Senate, *History of the Committee on the Judiciary, United States Senate, 1816-1981*, S. Doc. 97-18, 97th Cong., 1st sess. (Washington: GPO, 1982), p. iv.; also, U.S. Congress, Senate, *History of the Committee on Rules and Administration—United States Senate,* prepared by Floyd M. Riddick, Parliamentarian Emeritus of the Senate, S. Doc. 96-27, 96th Cong., 1st sess. (Washington: GPO, 1980). Riddick provided, on pp. 2 1-28, the full text of the general revision of the Senate rules, adopted in 1868, including, on p. 26, the following rule: "When nominations shall be made by the President of the United States to the Senate, they shall, unless otherwise ordered by the Senate, be referred to appropriate committees...."

63 For a more detailed numerical breakdown of Supreme Court nominations referred or not referred to the Senate Judiciary Committee (as well as a listing of the nominations since 1868 that were not referred), see CRS Report RL3 3225, *Supreme Court Nominations, 1789 - 2006: Actions by the Senate, the Judiciary Committee, and the President,* under heading "Referral of Nominations to Senate Judiciary Committee."

[64] Abraham, *Justices, Presidents, and Senators*, p. 33. One notable exception to this "unwritten rule," Abraham observed, was Franklin D. Roosevelt's "controversial selection" of Sen. Hugo L. Black (D-AL) in 1937, whose nomination was referred to the Judiciary Committee. Ibid., p. 34 (with discussion explaining various points of controversy over the Black nomination). See also Franklyn Waltman, "'Dark-Horse' Nomination of Alabaman Facing Study," *The Washington Post*, August 13, 1937, p. 1, which, on the day the Black nomination was received by the Senate, reported the following: "Efforts to have the Senate confirm the nomination immediately—a courtesy almost invariably granted when a member of the Senate is nominated for another post—were blocked by Senators Hiram Johnson (Republican), of California, and Edward R. Burke, Democrat, of Nebraska." Subsequently the Judiciary Committee, by a 13-4 vote, reported the Black nomination favorably, followed by a 63-16 vote of the Senate to confirm.

[65] Haynes's classic history of the Senate, published in 1938, noted what was then the "almost unbroken tradition that the nomination of a Senator or a former member of the Senate will be confirmed at once, without even being referred to a committee." Haynes cited, as illustrative, the contrasting experiences of two Supreme Court nominations in 1922— one of an attorney in private practice, Pierce Butler, which, prior to being confirmed, "was in controversy for nearly a month," the other of former Sen. George Sutherland (R-UT), which "without being referred to a committee, was confirmed by the Senate in open session within ten minutes after the name was received." George H. Haynes, *The Senate of the United States: Its History and Practice*, vol. 2 (Boston: Houghton Mifflin Company, 1938), p. 740.

[66] For a listing of the dates of actions by the Senate Judiciary Committee and full Senate on the Stone and Jackson nominations, see Table 1 in CRS Report RL3 3225, *Supreme Court Nominations, 1789 - 2006: Actions by the Senate, the Judiciary Committee, and the President.*

[67] "Nomination of Senator Byrnes To Be Associate Justice of the Supreme Court," *Congressional Record*, vol. 87, June 12, 1941, p. 5062.

[68] See "Senate Confirms Choice of Burton," *The New York Times*, September20, 1945, p. 44; "Senate Quickly Confirms Burton to Supreme Court," *Los Angeles Times*, September20, 1945, p. 4.

[69] For a narrative of the Judiciary Committee's consideration of the Minton nomination, including the nominee's declining a committee invitation that he testify before it, see James A. Thorpe, "The Appearance of Supreme Court Nominees Before the Senate Judiciary Committee," *Journal of Public Law*, vol. 18, 1969, pp. 380-385. (Hereafter cited as Thorpe, *Appearance of Supreme Court Nominees*.) See also Richard Baker, "October 1, 1949: Nominee Refuses to Testify," *The Hill*, September 24, 1997, in which the author, the Senate historian, characterized as a Senate custom "in decline" the practice of the Senate, prior to the Minton nomination of 1949, proceeding directly to consideration of a Supreme Court nominee, without referral to committee, when the nominee was a Senator.

It should be noted that not every Supreme Court nominee who was a Senator or former Senator when nominated was confirmed. While a Member of the Senate in 1853, George E. Badger of North Carolina was nominated to the Court but failed to gain Senate confirmation. Without being referred to the Judiciary Committee, the Badger nomination was considered by the Senate, which ultimately voted to postpone taking any action on the nomination. Of eight sitting U.S. Senators ever nominated to the Court, Badger was the only one who failed to receive Senate confirmation. See Epstein, *Supreme Court Compendium*, pp. 345-3 53, listing every Supreme Court nominee's occupational position at time of nomination. In addition to the Badger nomination, however, the nomination in 1828 of a *former* U.S. Senator, John J. Crittenden of Kentucky, failed to be confirmed, after first being referred to the Judiciary Committee. After the committee reported with the recommendation that the Senate not act on the Crittenden nomination during that session, the Senate voted to postpone taking action on the nomination. See Jacobstein and Mersky, *The Rejected*, pp. 23-23 and 57-59, for brief accounts of Crittenden and Badger nominations, respectively; also, see Table 4 in CRS Report RL3 1171, *Supreme Court Nominations Not Confirmed, 1789-2008,* for dates of committee and Senate actions, if any, on Supreme Court nominations not confirmed (including the Badger and Crittenden nominations).

70 Roy M. Mersky, Tarlton Law Library, University of Texas at Austin Law School, telephone conversation with the author, April 3, 2003. Professor Mersky and J. Myron Jacobstein have jointly compiled 19 volumes of Senate Judiciary Committee hearings transcripts and reports for Supreme Court nominations, starting with the Brandeis nomination in 1916 and carrying through the nomination of Stephen G. Breyer in 1994. See Roy M. Mersky and J. Byron Jacobstein, comp., *The Supreme Court of the United States: Hearings and Reports on Successful and Unsuccessful Nominations of Supreme Court Justices by the Senate Judiciary Committee, 1916-1994*, 19 vols. (Buffalo, N.Y.: William S. Hein & Co., 1977-1996).

71 See Thorpe, *Appearance of Supreme Court Nominees*, pp. 371-373.

72 The nominees in both cases were Senators. As discussed above, the Senate considered the Supreme Court nomination of Senator James F. Byrnes in 1941, without referral to the Judiciary Committee; also, as discussed above, while the Supreme Court nomination of Senator Harold H. Burton in 1945 was referred to the Judiciary Committee, the committee voted to report the nomination to the Senate without holding a confirmation hearing.

73 The nominees in both cases saw their nominations withdrawn before hearings were held. As discussed above, the Associate Justice nominations of John G. Roberts Jr. and Harriet E. Miers in 2005 were withdrawn before the start of scheduled hearings. Roberts, however, on the day his nomination was withdrawn, was re-nominated to be Chief Justice, and his second nomination received a hearing, before being reported by the Judiciary Committee and confirmed by the Senate.

74 See David Gregg Farrelly, "Operational Aspects of the Senate Judiciary Committee," (Ph.D. diss., Princeton University, 1949), pp. 184-199, in which author examined the procedures followed by the committee in its consideration of 15 Supreme Court nominations referred to it between 1923 and 1947. The author observed, on p. 192, that six of the 15 nominations were "confirmed without benefit of public hearings. Of the remaining nine nominations, full public hearings were used on two occasions, another appointee received a limited hearing, and six were given routine hearings. Only [John J.] Parker and [Felix] Frankfurter received full, open hearings." A "routine hearing," the author explained, on pp. 194-195, "differs from a full, open hearing in that a date is set for interested parties to appear and present evidence against confirmation. In other words, a meeting is scheduled without requests for one; an open invitation is extended by the committee for the filing of protests against an appointment."

75 In 1930, although Supreme Court nominee John J. Parker had communicated his willingness to testify, the Judiciary Committee voted against inviting him to do so. "Committee, 10 to 6, Rejects Parker," *The New York Times*, April 22, 1930, pp. 1, 23.

76 Thorpe, *Appearance of Supreme Court Nominees*, pp. 384-402.

77 Although the standard practice of the Judiciary Committee, prior to the O'Connor hearings in 1981, was to prohibit broadcast coverage of Supreme Court confirmation hearings, there was at least one notable exception to this practice during the early years of television broadcasting. Archival records of the Columbia Broadcasting System (CBS), obtained by the Congressional Research Service (CRS), show that, on February 26 and 27, 1957, the CBS television network filmed and broadcast a few minutes of the confirmation hearings of Supreme Court nominee William J. Brennan Jr. Much earlier, in 1939, in a deviation from its standard practice of not allowing film coverage of confirmation hearings, the Judiciary Committee permitted newsreel coverage of its hearing on Supreme Court nominee Felix Frankfurter. A newsreel excerpt from the Frankfurter hearing is included in a CRS video product; see CRS Report MM70010, *Supreme Court Appointment Process. Online Video and Audio. Video and Audio Tapes.*, by Denis Steven Rutkus.

[78] A study by the Congressional Research Service has found that, prior to 1967, a median number of nine days elapsed between Senate receipt of Supreme Court nominations and the Judiciary Committee's final vote on reporting them to the full Senate was nine. By contrast, from the Supreme Court nomination of Thurgood Marshall in 1967 through the nomination of Samuel A. Alito Jr. in 2005 (voted on by the committee in 2006), the median number of days elapsed between Senate receipt and final committee vote was 50. See CRS Report RL33225, *Supreme Court Nominations, 1789 - 2006: Actions by the Senate, the Judiciary Committee, and the President* (under subheading "Days from Senate Receipt to Final Committee Vote").

[79] Treated to date as public information are sections of the questionnaire that request biographical and financial disclosure information, as well as the nominee's responses to questions about the Constitution and the law. Treated to date by the committee as confidential (and not available to the media or the public) are the nominee's responses to more sensitive questions, such as whether he or she ever had been under a federal, state or local investigation for possible violation of a civil or criminal statute or had ever been sued by a client or other party.

[80] In this vein, when President George W. Bush was asked at a news conference whether he would release to the Judiciary Committee some or all of Supreme Court nominee Harriet E. Miers's legal work as White House counsel, he replied, "I just can't tell you how important it is for us to guard executive privilege in order for there to be crisp decision making in the White House." Richard W. Stevenson, "President, Citing Executive Privilege, Indicates He'll Reject Requests for Counsel's Documents," *The New York Times,* October 5, 2005 (accessed at http://www.nexis.com). For the views, against the backdrop of the Miers nomination, of a range of legal scholars on the extent to which a President may properly invoke executive privilege to deny the Senate the work product of a White House counsel nominated to the Supreme Court, see Marcia Coyle, "Battle Looming over Privilege," *The National Law Journal*, vol. 28, October 10, 2005, pp. 1, 21.

[81] CRS Report RL32935, *Congressional Oversight of Judges and Justices*, by Elizabeth B. Bazan and Morton Rosenberg (under heading "Judicial Nominations"), citing, as the basis for the above paragraph, a more detailed narrative of the 1986 conflict between the Judiciary Committee and the Reagan Administration over the Rehnquist documents provided in Louis Fisher, *The Politics of Executive Privilege* (Durham, NC: Carolina Academic Press, 2004), pp. 76-77.

Comparable requests from the Judiciary Committee have produced mixed results in the case of the three most recent Supreme Court nominees, whose backgrounds all included service in either the Department of Justice, the White House, or both. The Administration of President George W. Bush allowed the release of some documents from each of the three nominees' executive branch service, but refused the release of other documents. See, for example: David G. Savage and Henry Weinstein, "Files from Roberts' Reagan Years Are Released," *Los Angeles Times,* August 16, 2005, p. 12; William Branigin, "Bush Will Not Release All Miers Documents," *The Washington Post*, October 24, 2005 (accessed at http://www.washingtonpost.com); and Susan Milligan, "Top Democrats Question Alito's Credibility," *Boston Globe*, December 2, 2005 (accessed at http://www.nexis.com).

[82] The most recent appointee to the Court, Samuel A. Alito Jr., was reported to have met privately with more than 80 Senators between his nomination on November 10, 2005, and his confirmation on January 24, 2006. Jesse J. Holland (Associated Press), "Senate Moves Toward Alito's Confirmation," *Las Vegas Sun,* January 25, 2006 (accessed at http://www.lasvegassun.com). Of the two Supreme Court nominees who immediately preceded Alito, John G. Roberts Jr. and Harriet E. Miers, one paid numerous courtesy calls to Senate offices, while the other made fewer. "By the time Justice Roberts took the oath before the Senate Judiciary Committee, he had met with more than half of the 100 members of the Senate." By contrast, a week prior to the withdrawal of her nomination, Miers was reported to have met "with only about 25 senators," reportedly because the meetings that

had been held "had been fraught with misunderstandings and disagreements, giving ammunition to detractors .... " Charles Hurt, "Miers to End Her Meetings with Senators; Supreme Court Nominee Will Cram for Hearings," *The Washington Times*, October 21, 2005, p. A1.

[83] Traditionally, this evaluation role has been performed at the official invitation of the chair of the Senate Judiciary Committee. In 1947, the ABA committee was first invited by the committee's chair, Sen. Alexander Wiley (R-WI), to testify or file a recommendation on each judicial nomination receiving a hearing. Grossman, Joel B. *Lawyers and Judges: The ABA and the Politics of Judicial Selection* (New York: John Wiley and Sons Inc., 1966), p. 64. A central purpose of the Judiciary Committee, when it first invited the ABA committee to evaluate judicial nominees, was to "help insure that only the highest caliber [of] men and women ascended to the bench.... " Statement of Sen. Joseph R. Biden Jr., chair of the Senate Judiciary Committee, in U.S. Congress, Senate Committee on the Judiciary, *The ABA Role in the Judicial Nomination Process*, hearing,101st Cong., 1st sess., June 2, 1989 (Washington: GPO, 1991), p. 2.

[84] American Bar Association, *The ABA Standing Committee on the Federal Judiciary: What It Is and How It Works*, p. 9 (accessed April 26, 2007, at http://www.abanet.org/scfedjud/).

[85] Ibid., p. 2. In the ABA committee's investigation of a Supreme Court nominee, all 15 committee members take part in confidential interviews with practicing lawyers, judges, law professors and others "who are in a position to evaluate the prospective nominee's integrity, professional competence and judicial temperament." Ibid., p. 10. Meanwhile, teams of law school professors, as well as a separate team of practicing lawyers, examine the legal writing of a nominee. The results of these inquiries are forwarded to the full ABA committee.

[86] Ibid., p. 11. Invariably, a nominee's ABA rating receives prominent news coverage when it is sent to the Senate Judiciary Committee. In the past, a unanimously positive rating by the ABA committee almost always presaged a very favorable vote by the Judiciary Committee on the nominee as well. Conversely, a divided vote, or less than the highest rating, by the ABA committee usually served to flag issues about the nominee for the Senate Judiciary Committee to examine at its confirmation hearings, and these issues in turn have sometimes been cited by Senators on the Judiciary Committee who voted against reporting a nomination favorably to the Senate floor.

Since the inception of the ABA committee's evaluating role, most, but not all, Supreme Court nominees have received the highest ABA rating, while none has been found by a committee majority to be "not qualified." See generally CRS Report 96-446, *A Historical Overview* (available from author).

[87] The ABA committee was accused by some Senators, as well as by some conservative groups, of holding a liberal ideological bias. The committee's ratings of judicial nominees Robert H. Bork in 1987 and Clarence Thomas in 1991 in particular were cited as demonstrating prejudice against nominees with conservative judicial philosophies. The ABA rating of Bork was unusual, with 10 of the committee's 15 members finding the nominee "well qualified," four members rating him "not qualified," and one member voting "not opposed"—with no members voting for the intermediate "qualified" rating. For the Thomas nomination, 12 of the committee's 15 members found the nominee "qualified," two found him "unqualified," and one abstained. The mid-level rating by the 12-member majority was in contrast to the "well qualified" ratings that the ABA panel had unanimously given the two previous Supreme Court nominees, David H. Souter and Anthony M. Kennedy. See CRS Report 93-290, *The Supreme Court Appointment Process: Should It Be Reformed?* by Denis Steven Rutkus (available from author; hereafter cited as CRS Report 93 -290, *Should Appointment Process Be Reformed?*); also see CRS Report 96-446, *A Historical Overview* (available from author).

[88] "One cannot assume," Chairman Hatch wrote, "that a group as politically active as the ABA can at the same time remain altogether neutral, impartial and apolitical when it comes to

evaluating judicial qualifications." He added that "[p]ermitting a political interest group to be elevated to an officially sanctioned role in the confirmation process not only debases that process, but in my view, ultimately detracts from the moral authority of the courts themselves." He noted, however, that individual Senators were, "of course, free to give the ABA's ratings whatever weight they choose." Sen. Orrin G. Hatch, Letter to Colleagues on the Senate Judiciary Committee, February 24, 1997; see http://www.fed-soc.org/abaw3972.htm, also, Associated Press, "Hatch Hits ABA's Screening Role, *The Washington Times*, February 19, 1997, p. A4.

89 Audrey Hudson, "Democrats Want ABA To Vet Judges," *The Washington Times*, March 28, 2001, p. A4; "Democrats Say ABA's Vetting of Nominees Still Counts," *The Washington Post*, March 28, 2001, p. A5. During his chairmanship, Senator Leahy was critical of the Bush White House for declining to include the ABA in the pre- nomination evaluation process, "even though their decision adds to the length of time nominations must be pending before the Senate before they can be considered." Sen. Patrick J. Leahy, "Nomination of Morrison C. England, Jr. To Be United States District Judge for the Eastern District of California," *Congressional Record*, vol. 148, daily edition, August 1, 2002, p. S7814.

90 U.S. Congress, Senate Committee on the Judiciary, *Confirmation Hearing on the Nomination of John G. Roberts Jr. To Be Chief Justice of the United States,* 109th Cong., 1st sess., September 12-15, 2005 (Washington: GPO, 2005), pp. 451-455; U.S. Congress, Senate Committee on the Judiciary, *Confirmation Hearing on the Nomination of Samuel A. Alito Jr. To Be an Associate Justice of the Supreme Court of the United States,* 109th Cong., 2nd sess., January 9-13, 2006 (Washington: GPO, 2006), pp. 64 1-654. (Hereafter cited as Senate Judiciary Committee, *Confirmation Hearing on John G. Roberts*, and Senate Judiciary Committee, *Confirmation Hearing on Samuel A. Alito*.) The ABA committee unanimously gave both Roberts and Alito its "well qualified" rating.

91 Senate Judiciary Committee, *Confirmation Hearing on Samuel A. Alito*, p. 640.

92 For reportage on interest group support of, or opposition to, recent Supreme Court nominations during the pre- hearing stage, see David D. Kirkpatrick, "For Conservative Christians, Game Plan on the Nominee," *The New York Times,* August 12, 2005, p. 15; Jo Becker, "Television Ad War on Alito Begins; Liberals Try to Paint Court Pick as Tool of the Right Wing," *The Washington Post*, November 18, 2005, p. A3. For overviews of the role that interest groups played during an entire appointment process (from the point of Justice Sandra Day O'Connor's retirement announcement until the point that her successor, Samuel A. Alito Jr. was confirmed), see Lois Romano and Julie Eilperin, "Republicans Were Masters in the Race to Paint Alito; Democrats' Portrayal Failed to Sway the Public," *The Washington Post*, February 2, 2006, p. A1; David D. Kirkpatrick, "Paving the Way for Alito Began in Reagan Era," *The New York Times*, January 30, 2006, pp. A1, A18.

93 In this vein, a news account reported that *before* George W. Bush's announcement, on July 19, 2005, of his selection of John G. Roberts Jr. to succeed Associate Justice Sandra Day O'Connor, the "prospect of filling the first Supreme Court vacancy in 11 years" had "already mobilized political forces on both sides to raise vast financial resources in preparation for a struggle akin to a presidential campaign. From the moment O'Connor announced her retirement July 1, interest groups have been airing television and Internet advertising, blitzing supporters with e-mail, and pressuring elected officials to stand strong." Peter Baker and Jim VanderHei, "Bush Chooses Roberts for Court," *The Washington Post*, July 20, 2005, p. A1. (Hereafter cited as Baker, "Bush Chooses Roberts".)

94 Kirk Victor, "The Senate Showdown," *National Journal*, vol. 37, July 9, 2005, p. 2185.

95 Ibid., p. 2186.

96 Baker, "Bush Chooses Roberts," p. A1.

97 See, for example, "Hanna Rosin," "They're Fishing on the Hill, but It's No Vacation," *The Washington Post*, August 4, 2005, p. C1 (describing the work of the "Noms Unit," a "special unit of the 50-member Democratic staff of the Senate Judiciary Committee, which

in early August 2005, was tasked with investigating the background and past writings or statements of Supreme Court nominee John G. Roberts prior to Roberts's confirmation hearings scheduled to begin early the next month); see also Sheryl Gay Stolberg, "Out of Practice, Senate Crams for Battle over Court Nominee," *The New York Times*, July 8, 2005, pp. A1, A20 (describing the investigative and research roles of Republican staff on the Senate Judiciary Committee in early July 2005, as it prepared for President George W. Bush to select a nominee to succeed retiring Associate Justice Sandra Day O'Connor).

[98] See, for example, Seth Stern, "Leahy Says He Will Ask Roberts About So-Called Torture Memo," *CQ Today*, August 29, 2005 (accessed at http://www.cq.com); Gary Delsohn, "Feinstein to Seek Roberts' Abortion Views"), *Sacramento Bee*, August 25, 2005, p. A1 (accessed at http://www.nexis.com); Sen. Arlen Specter, Letter to Hon. John G. Roberts Jr., August 23, 2005. In his August 23, 2005, letter, Sen. Specter, then chair of the Judiciary Committee, began by stating, "Supplementing my letter on the Commerce Clause, this letter deals with Supreme Court decisions on the Americans with Disabilities Act (ADA), which I intend to ask you about at your confirmation hearing."

[99] Elisabeth Bumiller, "Lengthy Practices Prepare Court Nominee for his Senate Hearings," *The New York Times*, September 1, 2005, p. A11.

[100] For instance, in preparation for his confirmation hearings in September 2005, Associate Justice nominee John G. Roberts Jr. reportedly "participated in some 10 mock hearings of two to three hours each at the Justice Department, where administration lawyers and a revolving cast of Judge Roberts's colleagues and friends baited him with queries, including those they anticipated from the three Democratic senators who are widely expected to be toughest on the nominee.... " Ibid. After Judge Roberts's hearings were postponed (following the withdrawal of his Associate Justice nomination and then his re-nomination, this time to be Chief Justice), he apparently participated in even more mock hearings, for it was later reported that he "underwent at least a dozen murder boards in preparing for his hearings." Marcia Coyle, "Alito's 'Murder Board' a Mix of the Legal Elite," *The National Law Journal*, vol. 28, January 30, 2006, p. 7. Coyle, in the same article, reported that subsequently the most recent Supreme Court nominee, Samuel A. Alito Jr., also participated in a rigorous series of mock hearing sessions, in preparation for his confirmation hearings before the Senate Judiciary Committee in early January 2006. Alito, she noted, "was shepherded through all of the murder boards by a team that included Steve Schmidt, special advisor to the president in charge of the White House confirmation team, and Harriet Miers, counsel to the president." Coyle observed that the "well-handled U.S. Supreme Court nominee is now a fixture in the political process, and much of the credit goes to those so-called murder boards, or preparation sessions for the Senate confirmation hearings."

[101] The chair's opening statement might also express views on the nomination and confirmation process or on the nominee.

[102] The presenters often will include the Senators and, less frequently, Representatives from the state in which the nominee is a resident or the state in which the nominee was born or has resided for much of his or her life. Other presenters at recent Supreme Court confirmation hearings have included a former President (Gerard R. Ford, at the 1987 hearings for Robert H. Bork), the attorney general (William French Smith, at the 1981 hearings for Sandra Day O'Connor, and Edward Levi, at the 1975 hearings for John Paul Stevens); and a former attorney general (Griffin B. Bell, at the 1986 hearings for William H. Rehnquist).

[103] Almost invariably, the questioning is conducted exclusively by members of the committee. However, on at least two occasions in the 20th century, a Senator who was not a committee member was allowed to join in the questioning of the nominee. This first instance, in 1941, involved Sen. Millard E. Tydings (D-MD) at the confirmation hearings for nominee Robert H. Jackson; the second instance, in 1957, involved Sen. Joseph R. McCarthy (R-WI) at the confirmation hearings for nominee William J. Brennan Jr. See Thorpe, *Appearance of Supreme Court Nominees*, p. 378 (Jackson hearings) and p. 385 (Brennan hearings).

104 See CRS Report RL33059, *Proper Scope of Questioning of Supreme Court Nominees: The Current Debate*, by Denis Steven Rutkus; and CRS Report 90-429, *Questioning Supreme Court Nominees—A Recurring Issue*, by Denis Steven Rutkus (available from author).

105 See, for example, Charles Babington, "On Question of Nominee Questions, No Clear Answer," *The Washington Post*, July 28, 2005, p. A6, which examined the issue facing Senators on the Judiciary Committee, prior to confirmation hearings for Supreme Court nominee John G. Roberts Jr, "of what should be asked and answered—or not answered— in confirmation hearings later this summer."

106 See CRS Report 93-290, *The Supreme Court Appointment Process: Should It Be Reformed?* pp. 32-3 7 (available from author). See also William G. Ross, "The Questioning of Supreme Court Nominees at Senate Confirmation Hearings: Proposals For Accommodating the Needs of the Senate and Ameliorating the Fears of the Nominees," *Tulane Law Review*, vol. 62, November 1987, pp. 109-174.

107 Illustrative of such a concern was the following statement by nominee David H. Souter, at a September 14, 1990, hearing, explaining his refusal to answer a question concerning the issue of a woman's right, under the Constitution, to have an abortion: "Anything which substantially could inhibit the court's capacity to listen truly and to listen with as open a mind as it is humanly possible to have should be off-limits to a judge. Why this kind of discussion would take me down a road which I think it would be unethical for me to follow is something that perhaps I can suggest, and I will close with this question.

"Is there anyone who has not, at some point, made up his mind on some subject and then later found reason to change or modify it? No one has failed to have that experience. ... With that in mind can you imagine the pressure that would be on a judge who had stated an opinion, or seemed to have given a commitment in these circumstances to the Senate of the United States, and for all practical purposes, to the American people?" U.S. Congress, Senate Committee on the Judiciary, *Nomination of David Souter To Be Associate Justice of the Supreme Court of the United* States, hearings, 101st Cong., 2nd sess., September 13, 14, 17, 18 and 19, 1990 (Washington: GPO, 1991), p. 194.

108 As early as 1959, at the confirmation hearings for Supreme Court nominee Potter Stewart, there is a record of Judiciary Committee members differing among themselves as to appropriateness of certain areas of questioning for the nominee. During the hearings, Sen. Thomas C. Hennings Jr. (D-MO) raised a point of order about interrogating a nominee on his "opinion as to any of the questions or the reasoning upon decisions which have heretofore ... [been] handed down" by the Supreme Court. The point of order, however, was overruled by the committee's chair, Sen. James O. Eastland (D-MS), who stated the rule he would follow: "[I]f the nominee thinks that the question is improper, that he can decline to answer. And that when he declines, his position will be respected." L.A. Powe Jr., "The Senate and the Court: Questioning a Nominee," *Texas Law Review*, vol. 54, May 1976, p. 892, citing an unpublished transcript of the April 9 and 14, 1959, hearings of the Senate Judiciary Committee on the Supreme Court nomination of Potter Stewart, pp. 43-44.

109 That noncommittal replies by a Supreme Court nominee may be regarded differently by Senators on the Judiciary Committee appeared to be borne out at the confirmation hearings in September 2005 for Chief Justice nominee John G. Roberts Jr. In his first day of testimony, Roberts "was Delphic," according to one news analysis, "and his supporters and critics each ended the day saying his performance had hardened their enthusiasm or their doubts." Todd S. Purdum, "With His Goal Clear, the Nominee Provides a Profile in Caution During Questioning," *The New York Times,* September 14, 2005, p. 25.

110 Watson and Stookey, *Shaping America*, p. 150.

111 Ibid., p. 152.

112 See Stephen J. Wermiel, "Confirming the Constitution: The Role of the Senate Judiciary Committee," *Law and Contemporary Problems*, vol. 56, Autumn 1993, p. 141, in which the author maintained that, since the 1987 hearings on Supreme Court nominee Robert H. Bork, a purpose of Senators on the Judiciary Committee has been "to identify points of

constitutional concern and pursue those concerns with nominees, with the hope that, once confirmed, the new Justices will remember the importance of the core values urged on them by the senators or at least feel bound by the assurance they gave during their hearings."

113 Watson and Stookey, *Shaping America*, p. 155.

114 Sen. Joseph R. Biden Jr., "Reform of the Confirmation Process," remarks in the Senate, *Congressional Record*, vol. 138, June 25, 1992, p. 16320.

115 On February 15, 2005 (following a morning of public testimony by nominee John G. Roberts Jr.), the chair of the Judiciary Committee, Sen. Arlen Specter (R-PA), announced that the committee would immediately be going into executive session, "to ask the nominee on the record under oath about all investigative charges against the person if there were any." Such hearings, Chairman Specter said, "are routinely conducted for every Supreme Court nominee, even where there are no investigative issues to be resolved. In so doing, those outside the Committee cannot infer that the committee has received adverse confidential information about a nominee." Thirty-one minutes after proceeding to closed session, the committee reconvened in open session. Chairman Specter noted that the committee had reviewed "the background investigations on Judge Roberts, which were routine," and that he and the committee's ranking member, Sen. Patrick J. Leahy (D-VT), had been "delegated to report that there are no disqualifying factors." (The committee then proceeded to hear outside witnesses in open session.) Senate Judiciary Committee, *Confirmation Hearing on John G. Roberts*, p. 450. See also Senate Judiciary Committee, *Confirmation Hearing on Samuel A. Alito,* p. 640, where, after a brief executive session, Chairman Specter, in public session, announced that the committee had "reviewed confidential data on the background of Judge Alito, and it was all found to be in order."

116 Since its creation in 1816, the Judiciary Committee has reported to the Senate 106 Supreme Court nominations. Of the 106, seven were reported unfavorably—those of John Crittenden (1829), Ebenezer R. Hoard (1869), Stanley Matthews (1881), Lucius Q.C. Lamar (1888), William B. Hornblower (1894), John J. Parker (1930), and Robert H. Bork (1987). Two were reported without recommendation—those of Wheeler H. Peckham (1894) and Clarence Thomas (1991). See CRS Report RL33225, *Supreme Court Nominations, 1789 - 2006: Actions by the Senate, the Judiciary Committee, and the President* (under heading "Nominations Reported Out of Committee to Full Senate").

117 Of the 114 Supreme Court nominations referred to the Judiciary Committee since its establishment, only eight were not reported by the committee to the Senate. The final outcome for all eight nominees, however, was determined not by the failure of their nominations to be reported out of committee, but by action, or lack of action, taken outside the committee—by the Senate, Congress as a whole, or the President. For instance, the most recent nominee not reported out of committee was Harriett E. Miers, whose nomination, in 2005, was withdrawn by President George W. Bush before the start of scheduled confirmation hearings. For details regarding the failure of each of the eight nominations not reported, see CRS Report RL3 3225, *Supreme Court Nominations, 1789 - 2006: Actions by the Senate, the Judiciary Committee, and the President* (under heading "Nominations Not Reported Out of Committee").

118 Sen. Patrick J. Leahy and Sen. Orrin G. Hatch, "Dear Colleague" Letter, June 29, 2001, *Congressional Record*, daily edition, vol. 147, June 29, 2001, p. S7282.

119 From the 1960s to the present, the Judiciary Committee has reported 23 Supreme Court nominations to the Senate, 16 of which included transmittals of printed reports. During this time span, the seven Supreme Court nominations reported to the Senate without printed report were those of Byron W. White and Arthur J. Goldberg in 1962, Abe Fortas in 1965, Warren E. Burger in 1969, John Paul Stevens in 1975, John G. Roberts Jr. (for Chief Justice) in 2005, and Samuel A. Alito Jr. in 2006.

120 Rule 26, paragraph 10(c), *Standing Rules of the Senate.*

121 This argument, for instance, was raised in 1969, after the nomination of Warren E. Burger to be Chief Justice was reported by the Judiciary Committee to the Senate floor without a

printed report. During floor consideration of the nomination, three Senators expressed concern about the absence of a printed committee report. The Senators maintained that it was important for the Senate, when considering an appointment of this magnitude, to be able to consult a printed report from the Judiciary Committee that provided a breakdown of any recorded votes by the committee and an explanation of the committee's recommendation regarding the nominee. "The Supreme Court of the United States," debate in the Senate, *Congressional Record*, vol. 115, June 9, 1969, pp. 15174-15175 and 15192-15194. Shortly after this discussion, however, the Senate concluded debate on the Burger nomination and voted to confirm the nominee, 74-3.

[122] A written report ordinarily is produced within a week of the committee vote. On infrequent occasions, however, the report may entail weeks of preparation if the nomination is controversial or if the report is regarded as possibly crucial in influencing how the full Senate will vote on the nomination. In 1970, for instance, the committee submitted its written report on nominee Clement F. Haynsworth Jr. more than a month after voting 10-7 to recommend that Judge Haynsworth be confirmed. (Subsequently the full Senate rejected the Haynsworth nomination by a 55-45 vote.)

[123] Concern that vacancies on the Court be filled as expeditiously as possible appeared to figure in the decisions to report the two most recent Supreme Court nominees, John G. Roberts Jr. and Samuel A. Alito Jr., to the Senate without printed report. Dispensing with a written report for Roberts was briefly discussed on the Senate floor in July 29, 2005, the day his first nomination (for Associate Justice) was received by the Senate. (This nomination would later, on September 6, 2005, be withdrawn, with Roberts that same day re-nominated to be Chief Justice.) In a floor statement, the chair of the Judiciary Committee, Sen. Arlen Specter (R-Pa), described a joint agreement that he and the committee's ranking member, Sen. Patrick J. Leahy (D-VT), had reached with the Senate's party leaders concerning the scheduling procedures for the confirmation hearings on the Roberts nomination. The particulars of the agreement, Senator Specter said, were shaped by what he said was the Senate's "duty to have the nominee in place" on the Court by the start of its next term on October 3, 2005. In the list of particulars agreed to (including the start of hearings by a set date and the waiving by members of the Judiciary Committee of their right under committee rules to hold over the nomination for one week when first placed on the committee's executive agenda), Judiciary Committee members from both parties, Senator Specter said, "would waive their right to submit dissenting or additional or minority views to the committee report." "Hearings on Supreme Court Nominee John Roberts," *Congressional Record*, daily edition, vol. 151, July 29, 2005, p. S9420. Senator Leahy as well, in a floor statement immediately after Senator Specter, indicated that the joint agreement allowed for dispensing with a written committee report on the Roberts nomination: "And we recognize," Senator Leahy stated, "that nothing in the Senate or Judiciary Committee rules precludes the Senate from considering the nomination on the floor without a committee report." Ibid.

The scheduling of a Judiciary Committee vote on the Alito nomination, without a printed report by the committee to follow, also appeared to be grounded on concerns of acting as quickly on the nomination as possible. In Chairman Specter's initial announcement, on November 3, 2005, of a schedule for the Judiciary Committee and Senate floor action on the Alito nomination, he specified that floor action was to begin the day after the committee's vote (hence not allowing time for preparation of a printed report). Senator Specter observed that the Court was then in the midst of its October 2005 term, with the possibility of various cases already heard by the Court having to be reargued, if the departure of outgoing Justice Sandra Day O'Connor during the term were to result in 4-4 decisions. Thus, Senator Specter said, it was important to the Court for the Senate to act on the Alito nomination "as promptly as possible." "Senator Specter and Leahy Hold News Conference on Hearings for Supreme Court Justice Nominee Alito," CQ.Com Newsmaker Transcripts, November 3, 2005 (accessed at http://www.cq.com).

[124] The Senate disagreed with the Judiciary Committee's favorable assessment of a Supreme Court nominee three times in the 20th century, declining to confirm Supreme Court nominees Abe Fortas in 1968, Clement F. Haynsworth Jr. in 1969, and G. Harrold Carswell in 1970, even though their confirmation had been recommended by the committee. At least once in the 19th century, the Senate, in 1873, questioned a favorable committee report on a nominee to the Court, recommitting the nomination of George H. Williams to be Chief Justice; the nomination later was withdrawn by the President, without having been reported out a second time by the committee. A year later, in 1874, the nomination of Caleb Cushing to be Chief Justice failed to receive Senate confirmation after being reported favorably by the Judiciary Committee. Soon after the committee's action and in the face of growing Senate opposition, the nomination was withdrawn by President Ulysses S. Grant without, however, having received formal Senate consideration. See Jacobstein and Mersky, *The Rejected*, pp. 82-87 (Williams), pp. 87-89 (Cushing), pp. 125-137 (Fortas), pp. 141-147 (Haynsworth), and pp. 147-155 (Carswell).

[125] Specifically, the following three Supreme Court nominations, though reported out of committee without a favorable recommendation, nonetheless were confirmed by the Senate: Stanley Matthews (1881), by a 24-23 vote; Lucius Q.C. Lamar (1888), by a 32-28 vote; and Clarence Thomas (1991), by a 52-48 vote.

[126] For an examination of floor procedures used by the Senate in considering Supreme Court nominations, see CRS Report RL33247, *Supreme Court Nominations: Senate Floor Procedure and Practice, 1789-2006*, by Richard S. Beth and Betsy Palmer. The report examines the 146 Supreme Court nominations on which some form of formal proceedings took place on the Senate floor. It sketches the changing patterns of consideration that have been normal in successive historical periods since 1789, and, in considering all of the 146 nominations, discusses the kinds of dispositions that they received, the length of their floor consideration, and the kinds of procedural action taken during their consideration.

[127] "It is not in order for a Senator to move to consider a nomination that is not on the calendar, and except by unanimous consent a nomination on the calendar cannot be taken up until it has been on the calendar at least one day." Elizabeth Rybicki, CRS Report RL31980, *Senate Consideration of Presidential Nominations: Committee and Floor Procedure* (under heading Taking Up a Nomination"). The Senate may also discharge a matter from a committee, by motion or by unanimous consent.

[128] The latest issue of the Senate's Executive Calendar can be accessed electronically in the Legislative Information System of the U.S. Congress at *http://www.senate.gov/ legislative/ LIS/executive_calendar/xcalv.pdf.*

[129] See CRS Report RL3 1980, *Senate Consideration of Presidential Nominations: Committee and Floor Procedure.*

[130] In 1925, the full Senate for the first time considered a Supreme Court nomination—that of Harlan F. Stone to be an Associate Justice—in open session, waiving a rule requiring the chamber to consider nominations in closed session. In 1929, the Senate amended its rules to provide for debate on nominations in open session unless there were a vote to go into closed session. Thenceforth, it became the regular Senate practice to conduct debate on nominations, including those to the Supreme Court, in open session.

[131] The Senate has allowed gavel-to-gavel broadcast coverage of Senate floor debate since June 1986. The Senate's first floor debates on Supreme Court nominations ever to be televised were its September 1986 debates on the nominations of William H. Rehnquist to be Chief Justice and Antonin Scalia to be an Associate Justice.

[132] For instance, under a unanimous consent agreement propounded by Majority Leader Robert C. Byrd (D-WV), on October 21, 1987, the Senate proceeded immediately to consider the Supreme Court nomination of Robert H. Bork. Sen Robert C. Byrd, "Executive Session," remarks in the Senate, *Congressional Record*, vol. 133, October 21, 1987, p. 28654. Similarly, under a unanimous consent agreement requested by Majority Leader Bill Frist (R-TN) on January 25, 2006, the Senate proceeded immediately to consider the nomination

to the Court of Samuel A. Alito Jr Sen. Bill Frist, "Nomination of Samuel A. Alito, Jr., To Be an Associate Justice of the Supreme Court of the United States," remarks in the Senate, *Congressional Record*, vol. 152, daily edition, January 25, 2006, p. S35.

[133] For instance, on September 27, 1990, a unanimous consent agreement was propounded by Majority Leader George J. Mitchell (D-ME) providing for the Senate to proceed to the Supreme Court nomination of David H. Souter at 2:30 p.m., October 2. Sen. George J. Mitchell, "Nomination of David L. Souter To Be an Associate Justice of the Supreme Court of the United States," remarks in the Senate, *Congressional Record*, vol. 136, September 27, 1990, p. 26387. Likewise, on September 22, 2005, a unanimous consent agreement was obtained by Majority Leader Bill Frist (R-TN) providing for the Senate to proceed to the nomination of John G. Roberts Jr. to be Chief Justice of the United States, on September 26, 2005, "following the prayer and pledge" at 1 p.m. Sen. Bill Frist, "Orders for Monday, September 26, 2005," remarks in the Senate, *Congressional Record*, vol. 151, daily edition, September 22, 2005, p. S 10392.

[134] In this vein, Majority Leader George J. Mitchell (D-ME), on July 28, 1994, while the Senate was in legislative session, asked unanimous consent that at 9 a.m. on July 29, the Senate proceed to executive session to consider the Supreme Court nomination of Stephen G. Breyer. The unanimous consent request also specified that there be six hours of debate, after which the Senate, "without any intervening action on the nomination," would vote on whether to confirm. Sen. George J. Mitchell, "Unanimous-Consent Agreement," remarks in the Senate, *Congressional Record*, vol. 140, July 28, 1994, p. 18544. Likewise, unanimous consent requests limited the time for debate and set the date and time for Senate votes on the Supreme Court nominations of Ruth Bader Ginsburg (1993), Clarence Thomas (1991), Anthony M. Kennedy (1988), and Sandra Day O'Connor (1981).

[135] For example, a September 27, 1990, unanimous consent agreement, which provided for the Senate to proceed to the Supreme Court nomination of David H. Souter at 2:30 p.m., October 2, did not, however, also provide for a time limit on the debate, or for a vote at the end of that debate. Despite the absence of these provisions in the unanimous consent agreement, the Senate concluded its debate and voted to confirm, on the same day that it began debate on the Souter nomination, October 2. Likewise, the Senate on August 29, 1967, by unanimous consent, proceeded to consider the Supreme Court nomination of Thurgood Marshall, without also providing for a time limit on the debate, or for a vote certain on confirmation. "Supreme Court of the United States," *Congressional Record*, vol. 113, August 29, 1967, p. 24437. In the absence of such provisions, the Senate concluded debate on, and voted to confirm, the Marshall nomination the next day, August 30.

Also, the Senate, without providing for a vote on confirmation, may enter into one or more unanimous consent agreements, each with a time limit, to complete debate time and ultimately arrive at a time for a vote on confirmation. That was the scenario followed when the Senate in 2005 considered the nomination of John G. Roberts Jr. to be Chief Justice. Initial consideration of the Roberts nomination, on September 26, 2005, occurred pursuant to a unanimous consent agreement entered into on September 22, 2005. The agreement specified the precise amounts of time on September 26 to be allotted to the majority and minority party leaders or their designees for debate on the nomination, without, however, setting a date and time for a vote on confirmation. "Orders for Monday, September 26, 2005," *Congressional Record*, vol. 151, daily edition, September 22, 2005, p. S10392. Pursuant to three more UC agreements, further Senate consideration of the nomination followed, on September 27, 28, and 29, 2005, culminating in a 78-22 vote to confirm on September 29. (A complete chronology of Senate actions on the Roberts nomination, including all unanimous consent agreements reached on the nomination, can be accessed on the Legislative Information System's Nominations database at *http://www.congress.gov/nomis/.)*

[136] Charles Tiefer, *Congressional Practice and Procedure* (New York: Greenwood Press, 1989), p. 607. (Hereafter cited as Tiefer, *Congressional Practice and Procedure*.)

137 For full details on the cloture process, see CRS Report RL3 03 60, *Filibusters and Cloture in the Senate*, by Richard S. Beth and Stanley Bach.

138 For just as the motion to consider was a debatable question, permitting a filibuster by opponents, so, too, would be the question of whether to advise and consent to the nomination.

139 The vote on the motion to close debate on the motion to consider the Fortas nomination was 45-43, well short of the super-majority then required by Senate rules for passage of a "cloture motion" (prior to 1975, two-thirds of Senators present and voting). Shortly after the unsuccessful attempt at cloture, the Fortas nomination was withdrawn by President Lyndon B. Johnson.

140 Floyd M. Riddick and Alan S. Frumin, *Riddick's Senate Procedure*, S. Doc. 10 1-28, 101st Cong., 2nd sess. (Washington, GPO, 1992), pp. 94 1-942.

141 Tiefer, *Congressional Practice and Procedure*, p. 608.

142 See in following pages of this report, under the subheading "Filibusters and Motions To End Debate," discussion of the opposition, in January 2006, of some Senators to ending debate on the nomination of Samuel A. Alito Jr. to be an Associate Justice.

143 The single cloture vote needed to limit debate on the Alito nomination occurred five days after the Senate, on January 25, 2006, agreed by unanimous consent to consider it. Specifically, after continuing its consideration of the Alito nomination on January 26 and 27, the Senate on January 30 invoked cloture by a 72-25 vote, and confirmed Judge Alito to the Court the next day, by a vote of 58-42. See Charles Babington, "Senate To Vote on Alito Today; Confirmation Near as Filibuster Fails," *The Washington Post*, January 31, 2006, p. A1; Charles Babington, "Alito Is Sworn In on High Court," *The Washington Post*, February 1, 2006, p. A1.

144 "The advice-and-consent role of the Senate," one of its Members noted in 1994, "is something that we do not take lightly because this is the only opportunity for the people of this Nation to express whether or not they deem a nominee qualified to sit on the highest court in the land." Sen. Mark O. Hatfield, "Nomination of Stephen G. Breyer, of Massachusetts, To Be an Associate Justice of the Supreme Court of the United States," remarks in the Senate, *Congressional Record*, vol. 140, July 29, 1994, pp. 18692-18693.

145 See CRS General Distribution Memorandum, *Criteria Used by Senators To Evaluate Judicial Nominations*, by Denis Steven Rutkus, June 14, 2002 (available from author).

146 For example, during 1991 Senate debate on the Supreme Court nomination of Judge Clarence Thomas, the criterion of professional qualification was cited by both supporters and opponents of the nominee to explain their votes. A Senator supporting the Thomas nomination maintained that instead of the nominee's "philosophy on particular issues" which might come before the Supreme Court, the "more appropriate standard" was that the nominee "have outstanding legal ability and wide experience and meet the highest standards of integrity, judicial temperament, and professional competence." Judge Thomas, the Senator added, "clearly meets that standard." Sen. Frank H. Murkowski, "Nomination of Clarence Thomas to the Supreme Court," remarks in the Senate, *Congressional Record*, vol. 137, October 1, 1991, p. 24748. Other Senators, however, used the criterion of professional competence to find Judge Thomas unqualified. One, for example, found the nominee's "legal background and experience" inadequate and added that, if a President did not nominate to the court "well-qualified, experienced individuals, the American people have the right to expect that the members of the Senate will reject the nomination." Sen. Jeff Bingaman, "Justice Clarence Thomas," remarks in the Senate, *Congressional Record*, vol. 137, October 2, 1991, p. 24973.

147 During debate over the nomination of Clarence Thomas in 1991, these criteria were used both by Senators favoring the nomination and by others opposing it. One Senator in support of the nomination, for example, declared his desire to have "Supreme Court Justices who will interpret the Constitution and not attempt to legislate or carry out personal agendas from the bench." Sen. Richard C. Shelby, "Nomination of Judge Clarence Thomas To Be an

Associate Justice of the U.S. Supreme Court," remarks in the Senate, *Congressional Record*, vol. 137, October 1, 1991, p. 24703. By contrast, another Senator, explaining his opposition to confirming Judge Thomas, said that if Senators were "not confident that nominees possess a clear commitment to the fundamental constitutional rights and freedoms at the heart of our democracy, they should not be confirmed." Sen. Edward M. Kennedy, "Nomination of Clarence Thomas, of Georgia, To Be an Associate Justice of the Supreme Court of the United States," remarks in the Senate, *Congressional Record*, vol. 137, October 3, 1991, p. 25271.

148 "In addition to the obvious criteria any nominee for the Supreme Court ought to have—I suppose any nominee for any position on the judiciary ought to have—those of intellect, of integrity, and of judicial temperament, it is very appropriate of the Senate to inquire into a nominee's judicial philosophy. Of course, that includes the nominee's fidelity to the Constitution. It involves that nominee's understanding of the limited role of the courts, and it involves what I hope is a commitment to judicial restraint." Charles E. Grassley, "Supreme Court of the United States," remarks in the Senate, *Congressional Record*, vol. 139, August 2, 1993, p. 18133. Similarly evincing concern with both a nominee's professional qualification and his constitutional values was this 1991 Senate floor statement during debate on the nomination of Clarence Thomas: "When I face a Supreme Court nominee I have three questions: Is he or she competent? Does she or he possess the highest personal and professional integrity? And, third, will he or she protect and defend the core constitutional values and guarantees around free of speech, religion, equal protection of the law, and the right of privacy?" Sen. Barbara A. Mikulski, "Nomination of Clarence Thomas, of Georgia, To Be An Associate Justice of the Supreme Court of the United States," remarks in the Senate, *Congressional Record,* vol. 137, October 15, 1991, p. 26299.

149 Three political scientists wrote in 2002 that although "speculation about possible Supreme Court vacancies is usually met with much interest by court watchers, it is particularly intense at present due to the ideological balance of the current Court and the recent politics of the judicial confirmation process. Given the delicate ideological balance on the current Court, a single vacancy could produce a dramatic shift in the ideological direction of future rulings." Kenneth L. Manning, Bruce A. Carroll, and Robert A. Carp, "George W. Bush's Potential Supreme Court Nominees: What Impact Might They Have?," *Judicature*, vol. 85, May-June 2002, p. 278.

150 Linda Greenhouse, "Divided They Stand: The High Court and the Triumph of Discord," *The New York Times*, July 15, 2001, sec. 4, p. 1. Following the next two appointments to the Court—of Chief Justice John G. Roberts Jr. in 2005 and Associate Justice Samuel A. Alito Jr. in 2006—the proportion of 5-4 rulings by the Court increased. At the end of the Court's October 2006 term (the first full term with both Justices Roberts and Alito on the Court), Greenhouse reported that "[f]ully a third of the court's decisions, more than in any recent term, were decided by 5-to-4 margins. Most of those, 19 of 24, were decided along ideological lines, demonstrating the court's polarization whether on constitutional fundamentals or obscure questions of appellate procedure." Greenhouse added, "Of the ideological cases decided this term, the conservative majority, led by Chief Justice John G. Roberts Jr. and joined by Justices Antonin Scalia, Clarence Thomas and Samuel A. Alito Jr., prevailed in 13. The court's increasingly marginalized liberals—Justices John Paul Stevens, David H. Souter, Ruth Bader Ginsburg and Stephen G. Breyer—prevailed in only six...." Linda Greenhouse, "In Steps Big and Small, Supreme Court Moved Right," *The New York Times*, July 1, 2007, p. 1.

151 For example, during 1994 floor debate on the Supreme Court nomination of Stephen G. Breyer, one Senator said of the nominee's views: "Certainly in terms of an expansive definition of the Constitution, I have no doubt that Judge Breyer is going to make rulings that represent a different interpretation of the great document than I have and that people who share my views have. But I also believe that Judge Breyer's views are mainstream liberal views. I believe that anyone who voted for Bill Clinton knew or should have known

that the chances than anyone more conservative than Judge Breyer being nominated by Bill Clinton were almost zero." Sen. Phil Gramm, "Nomination of Stephen G. Breyer, of Massachusetts, To Be an Associate Justice of the Supreme Court of the United States," remarks in the Senate, *Congressional Record*, vol. 140, July 29, 1994, pp. 18671-18672.

152 A key to Senate division over the nomination of Samuel A. Alito Jr. in 2005-2006, it can be argued, was a widespread perception that confirmation of Alito would change the ideological balance of the Court in that he might align in decisions with Justices whose views were regarded by some as conservative. See, for example, Seth Stern and Keith Perine, "Alito Confirmed After Filibuster Fails," *CQ Weekly,* vol. 64, February 6, 2006, p. 340 (characterizing Alito's confirmation, "by a mostly party-line vote of 58-42," as "the culmination of years of planning by conservatives to move the court to the right"); also, "A Supreme Nomination," *The Washington Times*, November 1, 2005, p. A1 8 (editorial describing the nomination as "the moment conservatives have been waiting for" and predicting a "confirmation battle" in the Senate).

Earlier, in 1987, Senate concern with a nominee's judicial philosophy was also especially heightened when President Reagan nominated appellate court judge Robert H. Bork to the Court. The nomination sparked immediate controversy, and polarized the Senate generally along party lines, in large part because of the nominee's judicial philosophy of "original intent" and the perception that he had been nominated by President Reagan to move the Court in the future in what was characterized as a more conservative direction. For analysis of how central an issue Judge Bork's judicial philosophy was in the Senate confirmation battle, see John Massaro, *Supremely Political: The Role of Ideology and Presidential Management in Unsuccessful Supreme Court Nominations.* (Albany, NY: State University of New York Press, 1990), pp. 159-193. (Hereafter cited as Massaro, *Supremely Political.*)

In a Senate floor statement shortly after the Bork nomination was made, the then-chair of the Senate Judiciary Committee, Sen. Joseph R. Biden, Jr. (D-DE), faulted the President for his choice. Senator Biden declared that when a President selects nominees "with more attention to their judicial philosophy and less attention to their detachment and statesmanship," a Senator "has not only the right but the duty to respond by carefully weighing the nominee's judicial philosophy and the consequences for the country." The Senate, he continued, had both the right and the duty to raise political and judicial "questions of substance," for "we are once again confronted with a popular President's determined attempt to bend the Supreme Court to his political ends." Sen. Joseph R. Biden Jr., "Advice and Consent: The Right and Duty of the Senate To Protect the Integrity of the Supreme Court," remarks in the Senate," *Congressional Record*, vol. 133, July 23, 1987, p 20913 (first quote) and p. 20915 (second quote).

Various Senators who favored Judge Bork's confirmation, however, disagreed with Senator Biden regarding the importance of the nominee's judicial philosophy. Some expressed a preference for a narrower scope of Senate inquiry, focusing on Judge Bork's legal competence and character. Others considered Judge Bork's judicial philosophy and views of the Constitution appropriate areas of inquiry, but the crucial determination for the Senate to make in these areas, they argued, was whether his views fell within a broad range of acceptable thinking, not whether individual senators agreed with those views. Further, some Senators maintained, to evaluate a nominee according to political or judicial philosophy, or to vote to confirm only if Senators agreed with the nominee's views, would politicize the Supreme Court and undermine its independence of the legislative branch. See CRS Report 87-761, *Senate Consideration of the Nomination of Robert H. Bork To Be a Supreme Court Associate Justice—Background and an Overview of Issues*, by Denis Steven Rutkus (available from author), pp. 25-27.

153 See Watson and Stookey, *Shaping America*, pp. 191-195, for discussion of how a relatively few number of Senators may serve as "cues" to other Senators during the consideration of controversial Supreme Court nominations.

[154] Illustrative of this, during 1991 Senate debate over the Clarence Thomas nomination, Sen. Frank H. Murkowski (R- AK) stated, "I have heard from a number of Alaskans and visited with them last week during our recess. Many have gone back and forth during the testimony, but now the hearings are concluded, and they are telling me by a substantial majority that they favor the confirmation of Judge Thomas by this body." Sen. Frank H. Murkowski, "Nomination of Clarence Thomas, of Georgia, To Be An Associate Justice of the Supreme Court of the United States," remarks in the Senate, *Congressional Record*, vol. 137, October 15, 1991, p. 26300.

[155] See Watson and Stookey, *Shaping America*, pp. 198-199.

[156] In recent decades, for instance, Presidents and Senators at various times have endorsed the goal of increasing the representation of women and persons of minority ethnicity in the lower courts, as well as on the Supreme Court, to make the judiciary more representative of the nation's population.

[157] Concern for adequate representation of women on the Court, for instance, was expressed by some Senators after President George W. Bush nominated Samuel A. Alito Jr. to succeed retiring Justice Sandra Day O'Connor. (President Bush had nominated Alito after withdrawing his earlier nomination of White House counsel Harriet E. Miers to succeed Justice O'Connor.) Confirmation of Alito, it was widely noted, would leave the Court with only one woman member, Justice Ruth Bader Ginsburg. In this context, Sen. Barbara A. Mikulski (D-MD), during January 25, 2006, floor debate on the Alito nomination, remarked, "After Harriet Miers was withdrawn, who did they give us? Certainly, I think in all of the United States of America there was a qualified woman who could have been nominated to serve on the Court." Sen. Barbara A. Mikulski, "Nomination of Samuel A. Alito Jr. To Be an Associate Justice on the Supreme Court of the United States," remarks in the Senate, *Congressional Record*, daily edition, vol. 152, January 25, 2006, p. S66.

[158] President George W. Bush, for instance, received bipartisan praise for personally, and through his aides, consulting widely with Members of the Senate, over a several week period, prior to nominating John G. Roberts Jr. to the Court in 2005. See, for example, the remarks of Majority Leader Bill Frist (R-TN), in "Supreme Court Confirmation Process," remarks in the Senate, *Congressional Record*, daily edition, vol. 151, July 12, 2005, pp. S809 1-S8092, and of Senate Democratic Leader Harry Reid (D-NV) in "Pressing Issues," remarks in the Senate, *Congressional Record*, daily edition, vol. 151, July 11, 2005, pp. S7945-S7946. By contrast, President Bush's announcement of Samuel A. Alito Jr. on October 31, 2005, as a Court nominee, occurring four days after the withdrawal of a previous nominee to the same position (Harriet E. Miers), was faulted by some Senators as a selection made with little concern for consultation with Senators. Instead of an invitation to the White House, Senator Reid stated, "I received nothing more than a pro forma telephone call from the President's Chief of Staff, telling me he had selected Judge Alito about an hour before he announced the nomination." Sen. Harry Reid, "The Nomination of Judge Alito," remarks in the Senate,"*Congressional Record,* daily edition, November 16, 2005, p. S12874.

[159] Among those Senators supporting the nomination, one declared that he strongly believed "that a nominee comes to the Senate with a presumption in his favor. Accordingly, opponents of the nominee must make the case against him, especially since Judge Thomas has been confirmed to positions of great trust and responsibility on four separate occasions." Sen. Strom Thurmond, "Supreme Court of the United States," remarks in the Senate, *Congressional Record*, vol. 137, October 3, 1991, p. 25257. Another Senator stated that while his vote in favor of Judge Thomas was not "cast without some doubt, ... I have tried to insist on every judicial nomination of every President that I would give both the President and the nominee the benefit of the doubt." Sen. Wyche Fowler Jr., "Supreme Court of the United States," remarks in the Senate, *Congressional Record*, vol. 137, October 3, 1991, p. 25270.

[160] During the Thomas nomination debate, for example, one Senator declared that "[i]n the selection of a person to serve on the Nation's highest court, in my view, the Senate is an

equal partner with the President. The President is owed no special deference, and his nominee owed no special presumptions. We owe the public our careful and thorough consideration and our independent judgement." Sen. Frank R. Lautenberg, "Against the Confirmation of Clarence Thomas," remarks in the Senate, *Congressional Record*, vol., 137, September27, 1991, p. 24449. Likewise, another Senator maintained that, on "a question of such vast and lasting significance, where the course of our future for years to come is riding on our decision, the Senate should give the benefit of the doubt to the Supreme Court and to the Constitution, not to Judge Clarence Thomas." Sen. Edward M. Kennedy, "Nomination of Clarence Thomas, of Georgia, To Be an Associate Justice of the Supreme Court of the United States," remarks in the Senate, *Congressional Record*, vol. 137, October 15, 1991, p. 26290.

[161] For the complete record of the June 26, 2001 hearing, entitled "Judicial Nominations 2001: Should Ideology Matter?" see pp. 1-109 in U.S. Congress, Senate Committee on the Judiciary, Subcommittee on Administrative Oversight and the Courts, *The Judicial Nomination and Confirmation Process*, hearings, 1 07th Cong., 1st sess., June 26 & September 4, 2001 (Washington: GPO, 2002).

[162] Ibid., pp. 2-3.

[163] Ibid., p. 30. Soon thereafter, on September 4, 2001, the same Senate Judiciary subcommittee held a hearing on a related issue involving judicial nominations—namely, does the "burden of proof" lie with the nominee, to demonstrate that he or she merits appointment to the federal bench, or with Senate opponents, to demonstrate that the nominee is unfit for confirmation? The hearing, entitled "The Senate's Role in the Nomination and Confirmation Process: Whose Burden?," featured two panels of witnesses, some arguing for, and others against, placing the burden of proof on the nominee. See Ibid., pp. 111-218, for the complete record of the September 4 hearing.

[164] Much of the discussion under this subheading is based on, and borrows extensively from, CRS Report RL32878, *Cloture Attempts on Nominations*, by Richard S. Beth and Betsy Palmer.

[165] As discussed earlier, however, the Senate may set time limits on such debates by unanimous consent.

[166] See discussion earlier in this report, regarding debatable motions and filibusters, under subheading "Bringing the Nomination to the Floor."

[167] Prior to 1975, the majority required for cloture was two-thirds of Senators present and voting, a quorum being present. CRS Report RL32878, *Cloture Attempts on Nominations* (under heading "Historical Development of Cloture Attempts on Nominations").

[168] It has only been since 1949, under Senate rules, that cloture could be moved on nominations. Prior to 1949, dating back to the Senate's first adoption of a cloture rule in 1917, cloture motions could be filed only on legislature measures. Ibid.

[169] For the Senate's debate on the Fortas nomination immediately prior to the vote on the motion to close debate, see "Supreme Court of the United States," *Congressional Record*, vol. 114, October 1, 1968, pp. 28926-28933.

[170] For the Senate's debate on the Rehnquist nomination immediately prior to the vote on the motion to close debate, see "Cloture Motion," *Congressional Record*, vol. 117, December 10, 1971, pp. 46110-46117.

[171] The Senate, on December 10, 1971, confirmed the Rehnquist nomination by a vote of 68-26, after voting 22-70 to reject a motion that a vote on the nomination be deferred until January 18, 1972. *Congressional Record*, vol. 117, December 10, 1971, p. 46121 (vote on motion to defer) and p. 46197 (confirmation vote).

[172] "Nomination of William H. Rehnquist To Be Chief Justice of the United States," *Congressional Record*, vol. 132, September17, 1986, pp. 23729-23739.

[173] "Cloture Motion," *Congressional Record,* January 26, 2006, daily edition, vol. 152, p. S197.

[174] "Nomination of Samuel A. Alito, Jr., To Be an Associate Justice of the Supreme Court of the United States," *Congressional Record*, January 30, 2006, daily edition, vol. 152, pp. S260-S308.

[175] Matthew Tully, "Senators Won't Rule Out Filibuster of High Court Nominees," *CQ Daily Monitor*, March 21, 2002, p. 7.

[176] Ibid.

[177] See CRS Report RL31868, *U.S. Circuit and District Court Nominations by President George W. Bush During the 107th-109th Congresses*, by Denis Steven Rutkus, Maureen Bearden, and Kevin M. Scott (listing, in Appendix 3, all of President Bush's circuit court nominations during the 108th Congress, including votes in the Senate on motions to end debate on 10 of the nominations).

[178] In March 2005, a Congressional Research Service report noted that in "recent years, final Senate action on several presidential nominations for federal judgeships has been impeded by filibusters or threatened filibusters." As a result, "some leading Senators have called for the Senate to change its procedures to prevent filibusters, or make them harder to sustain, at least on this class of business." CRS Report RL32843, *"Entrenchment" of Senate Procedure and the "Nuclear Option" for Change: Possible Proceedings and Their Implications*, by Richard S. Beth (under heading "Introduction").

[179] Senate Republican leaders announced that their move to change Senate precedents to bar filibusters against judicial nominations would occur in conjunction with their efforts to close floor debate on the nomination of Priscilla Owen to be a U.S. circuit court of appeals judge. (An earlier nomination of Owen to the same judgeship, during the 108th Congress, had been filibustered successfully by Senate Democrats four times.) Keith Perine and Daphne Retter, "Judicial Showdown Starts with Owen," *CQ Today*, vol. 41, May 18, 2005.

[180] Charles Babington and Shailagh Murray, "A Last-Minute Deal on Judicial Nominations," *The Washington Post*, May 24, 2005, pp. A1, A4. See also CRS Report RS22208, *The "Memorandum of Understanding": A Senate Compromise on Judicial Filibusters*, by Walter J. Oleszek; and CRS Report RL33094, *Congress and the Courts: Current Policy Issues*, by Walter J. Oleszek (under headings "The Bipartisan Agreement: A Memorandum of Understanding" and "Diverse Definitions of 'Extraordinary Circumstances'").

[181] Several Senate Democrats, it was reported in 2002, had said "they would consider staging a filibuster if President Bush nominates to the high court a conservative not to their liking." Matthew Tully, "Senators Won't Rule Out Filibuster of High Court Nominees," *CQ Daily Monitor*, March 21, 2002, p. 7. More recently, in June 2003, another Democratic Senator declared that he would filibuster any Supreme Court nominee that he found objectionable based on certain specified criteria. Adam Nagourney, "Senator Ready To Filibuster over Views of Court Pick," *The New York Times*, June 21, 2003, p. A13.

[182] See, for example, Jonathan Allen, "Dems Hint at Filibuster," *The Hill*, November 1, 2005 (accessed at http://www.hillnews.com/); also,, Charles Hurt, "Alito Nomination to Test 'Gang of 14"; GOP Sees No Reason to Allow Filibuster," *The Washington Times*, November 2, 2005, pp. A1, A12.

[183] See Seth Stern and Keith Perine, "Alito Confirmed after Filibuster Fails," *CQ Weekly*, vol. 64, February 6, 2006, pp. 340-341.

[184] See David D. Kirkpatrick, "Alito Clears Final Hurdle for Confirmation to Court," *The New York Times*, January 31, 2006, p. 1. The article reported that, on the afternoon before the cloture vote, the 14 Senators who were part of the May 23, 2005, agreement met and "agreed unanimously that the 'extraordinary circumstances' stipulation [to justify a filibuster] did not apply in Judge Alito's case" and that a week earlier "more than the requisite 60 senators had committed to opposing a filibuster."

[185] "The Filibuster That Wasn't," *The Washington Post*, February 5, 2006, p. B6.

[186] The wording of the question is dictated by Rule XXXI, paragraph 1, *Standing Rules of the Senate* (accessed at http://rules.senate.gov/senaterules/rule31.php), which provides that "the final question on every nomination shall be, 'Will the Senate advise and consent to this nomination?"

[187] See CRS Report RL3 1980, *Senate Consideration of Presidential Nominations: Committee and Floor Procedure* (under heading "Consideration and Disposition"). This quorum

requirement is derived from Article I, Section 5, Clause 1 of the Constitution, which states in part that "a Majority of each [House] shall constitute a Quorum to do Business...." Hence, the quorum for conducting business in a Senate of 100 Members is 51 Senators.

188 See Table 2 in CRS Report RL3 3225, *Supreme Court Nominations, 1789 - 2006: Actions by the Senate, the Judiciary Committee, and the President.* The table breaks down numerically into four historical periods the 133 votes cast by the Senate, from 1789 to 2006, on whether to confirm particular Supreme Court nominees. The number of Senate votes within each historical period, in turn, is broken down according to whether they were voice votes or votes by unanimous consent on the one hand, or roll-call votes on the other.

189 The most recent voice votes by the Senate on Supreme Court nominations were those confirming Abe Fortas in 1965 (to be an Associate Justice) and Arthur J. Goldberg and Byron R. White, both in 1962. Of the 133 Senate votes cast in all, from 1789 to 2006, on whether to confirm a Supreme Court nominee, 60 were done by roll-call votes, and the other 73 by voice votes or unanimous consent. See again Table 2 in CRS Report RL3 3225, *Supreme Court Nominations, 1789 - 2006: Actions by the Senate, the Judiciary Committee, and the President.*

190 The closest roll calls ever cast on Supreme Court nominations were the 24-23 vote in 1881 confirming Stanley Matthews, the 25-26 vote in 1861 rejecting a motion to proceed to consider the nomination of Jeremiah S. Black, and the 26-25 Senate vote in 1853 to postpone consideration of the nomination of George E. Badger. Since the 1960s, the closest roll calls on Supreme Court nominations were the 52-48 vote in 1991 confirming Clarence Thomas, the 45-5 1 vote in 1970 rejecting G. Harrold Carswell, the 45-55 vote in 1969 rejecting Clement Haynsworth Jr., the 58-42 vote in 2006 confirming Samuel A. Alito Jr., the 42-58 vote in 1987 rejecting Robert H. Bork, and the 65-33 vote confirming William H. Rehnquist to be Chief Justice in 1986. Also noteworthy was the 45-43 vote in 1968 rejecting a motion to end debate on the nomination of Abe Fortas to be Chief Justice; however, the roll call was not as close as the numbers by themselves suggested, since passage of the motion required a two-thirds vote of the Members present and voting. See Table 1 in CRS Report RL3 3225, *Supreme Court Nominations, 1789 - 2006: Actions by the Senate, the Judiciary Committee, and the President.*

191 The most lopsided of these votes were the unanimous roll calls confirming Morrison R. Waite to be Chief Justice in 1874 (63-0), Harry A. Blackmun in 1970 (94-0), John Paul Stevens in 1975 (98-0), Sandra Day O'Connor in 1981 (99-0), Antonin Scalia in 1986 (98-0), and Anthony M. Kennedy in 1988 (97-0); and the near-unanimous votes confirming Noah H. Swayne in 1862 (38-1), Warren E. Burger in 1969 to be Chief Justice (74-3), Lewis F. Powell Jr. in 1971 (89-1), and Ruth Bader Ginsburg in 1993 (96-3). See again Table 1 in CRS Report RL33225, *Supreme Court Nominations, 1789 - 2006: Actions by the Senate, the Judiciary Committee, and the President.*

192 The five most recent Senate confirmation votes on Supreme Court nominations were those for nominees Clarence Thomas in 1991, Ruth Bader Ginsburg in 1993, Stephen G. Breyer in 1994, John G. Roberts Jr. in 2005, and Samuel A Alito Jr. in 2006. In each instance, Senators remained at their desks during the calling of the roll.

193 S.Res. 480, approved by the Senate on October 11, 1984, provided: "Resolved, That it is a standing order of the Senate that during yea and nay votes in the Senate, each Senator shall vote from the assigned desk of the Senator." See U.S. Congress, Senate, *Senate Manual Containing the Standing Rules, Orders, Laws , and Resolutions Affecting the Business of the United States Senate,* S. Doc. 107-1, 107th Cong., 1st sess. (Washington: GPO. 2002), p. 151.

194 "Senators are required to vote from their desks, but this requirement rarely is enforced. On occasion, when a vote of special constitutional importance, such as a vote to convict in an impeachment trial, is about to begin, the majority leader will ask all Senators to come to the floor before the vote begins and then to vote from their desks...." CRS Report 96-452,

Voting and Quorum Procedures in the Senate, by Betsy Palmer (under heading "Conducting Rollcall Votes").

[195] Immediately prior to the Senate's roll-call vote in 1994 on whether to confirm Stephen G. Breyer to be an Associate Justice, Majority Leader George J. Mitchell (D-ME) stated to his colleagues on the floor that "it has been the practice that votes on Supreme Court nominations are made from the Senator's desk. I ask that Senators cast their votes from their desks during this vote." *Congressional Record*, vol. 140, July 29, 1994, p. 18704. Again, in 2006, moments before the Senate's vote on nominee Samuel A. Alito Jr., the importance of a Supreme Court nomination was cited by the Senate's majority leader in applying the Senate rule that Members vote from their desks on a roll-call votes: "So, momentarily, we will vote from our desks, a time-honored tradition that demonstrates, once again, how important and consequential every Member takes his duty under the Constitution to provide advice and consent on a Supreme Court nomination and to give the nominee the fair up-or-down vote he deserves." Sen. Bill Frist, "Nomination of Judge Samuel Alito to the U.S. Supreme Court," remarks in the Senate, *Congressional Record,* daily edition, vol. 152, January 31, 2006, p. 348.

[196] "According to Senate Rule XXXI, any Senator who voted with the majority has the option of moving to reconsider a vote on the nomination. The motion to reconsider is in order on the day of the vote or the next two days the Senate meets in executive session. The motion is made in executive session or, by unanimous consent, 'as in executive session.'" CRS Report RL3 1980, *Senate Consideration of Presidential Nominations: Committee and Floor Procedure* (under subheading "Reconsideration").

[197] For example, immediately after the votes to confirm David Souter in 1990, Clarence Thomas in 1991, John G. Roberts Jr. in 2005, and Samuel A. Alito Jr. in 2006, a motion in each case was made to reconsider the vote, followed by a motion "to lay that motion on the table," which was agreed to without objection by the Senate. See *Congressional Record*, vol. 136, October 2, 1990, p. 26997; vol. 137, October 15, 1991, p. 26354; vol. 151 (daily edition), September 29, 2005, p. S 10650; and vol. 152 (daily edition), January 31, 2006, p. S348.

[198] By unanimous consent, the Senate in 1993 and 1994, for example, agreed that the motion to reconsider be tabled upon confirmation, respectively, of the Supreme Court nominations of Ruth Bader Ginsburg and Stephen G. Breyer. See "Unanimous-Consent Agreement," *Congressional Record*, vol. 139, July 30, 1993, p. 17996, and "Unanimous- Consent Agreement," *Congressional Record*, vol. 140, July 28, 1994, p. 18544.

[199] CRS Report RL3 3225, *Supreme Court Nominations, 1789 - 2006: Actions by the Senate, the Judiciary Committee, and the President* (under heading "Final Action by the Senate or the President").

[200] CRS Report RL3 1171, *Supreme Court Nominations Not Confirmed, 1789-2008* (under heading "Summary of Unsuccessful Nominations"). The six individuals who were confirmed after being re-nominated, it will be recalled (from "Background" section, above), were William Paterson (1793). Roger B. Taney (1835), Stanley Matthews (1881), Pierce Butler (1922), John W. Harlan II (1954-1955), and John G. Roberts Jr. (2005).

[201] A more detailed table about each unsuccessful Supreme Court nomination is available in CRS Report RL3 1171, *Supreme Court Nominations Not Confirmed, 1789-2008.* Specifically, Table 4 in that report provides, for each unconfirmed Supreme Court nomination, the dates of relevant activity and votes in the Judiciary Committee as well as in the full Senate.

[202] See section in CRS Report RL3 1171, *Supreme Court Nominations Not Confirmed, 1789-2008* (under heading "Factors Behind Unsuccessful Nominations").

[203] For a lengthy bibliographic listing of scholarly sources that deal directly with the factors associated with unsuccessful Supreme Court nominations, see Massaro, *Supremely Political*, p. 218, n. 4.

[204] Abraham, *Justices, Presidents and Senators*, p. 28. Abraham's book, it should be noted, predates the unsuccessful nomination of Harriet E. Miers to the Court in 2005. For a discussion of factors that appeared to contribute to the failure of the Miers nomination to be

confirmed, see CRS Report RL3 1171, *Supreme Court Nominations Not Confirmed, 1789-2008* (under heading "Application of the Factors to the Miers Nomination") and Greenburg, *Supreme Conflict,* pp. 277-282.

[205] Massaro, *Supremely Political*, p. xi.

[206] Massaro, in *Supremely Political*, p. 139, wrote that a nomination made "during the last full year of a president's term or in the interregnum period after a new chief executive has been elected presents an additional factor upon which to base opposition to confirmation." The vacancy's "unfavorable timing," he explained, can "generate opposition of its own as well as activate the otherwise dormant ideological resistance, significantly increasing the likelihood of the Senate's refusal to confirm. This is readily seen in the remarkably high refusal rate of seventy-one percent (ten of fourteen) for such nominations when they are also forwarded to a Senate in which the chief executive's party is in the minority."

[207] The Fortas, Haynsworth, Carswell, and Bork nominations, one scholar wrote, were all instances in which Presidents failed to give enough care to presidential management of the confirmation process. In the cases of the Fortas, Haynsworth and Carswell nominations, he wrote, opposition was "needlessly increased" when Presidents, without ensuring that "positive relationships with senators" were maintained, nominated individuals who were "vulnerable to non-ideological, non-partisan charges." Massaro, *Supremely Political*, pp. 140-142. In nominating Robert H. Bork, President Reagan, according to the author, fell short in exercising presidential management by failing to anticipate potential opposition in the Senate to a "controversial individual" at "a time demanding a careful and conciliatory course." Ibid., p. 190.

For a contrasting criticism of the Reagan Administration's strategy for the Bork nomination (one not faulting President Reagan for the fact that he chose, in Bork, a highly controversial nominee), see Greenburg, *Supreme Conflict*, who, at p. 50, wrote that the Reagan White House "never developed a strategy to sell Robert Bork to the senators and the American people" and "inexplicably chose not to defend Bork's constitutional approach to the law" or to launch the "ideological battle" that "many conservatives wanted to have." The result, according to Greenburg, was that Bork opponents "were able to define the nominee as a Stone Age extremist who would turn the clock back on civil rights for women and minorities."

[208] Besides the successful attempts in the Senate to recommit the nominations of George H. Williams as Chief Justice in 1873 and Harlan F. Stone as Associate Justice in 1925 (both discussed in this report), six other unsuccessful attempts to recommit Supreme Court nominations were recorded—specifically, the motions to recommit President Ulysses S. Grant's nomination of Joseph P. Bradley in 1870, President Warren G. Harding's nomination of Pierce Butler in 1922, President Herbert Hoover's nomination of Charles Evans Hughes as Chief Justice in 1930, President Franklin D. Roosevelt's nomination of Hugo L. Black in 1937, President Harry S. Truman's nomination of Sherman Minton in 1949, and President Richard M. Nixon's nomination of G. Harrold Carswell in 1970. *Congressional Quarterly Almanac, 1970*, vol. 26 (Washington: Congressional Quarterly, Inc., 1971), p. 161.

[209] U.S. Congress, Senate, *Journal of the Executive Proceedings of the Senate of the United States of America*, vol. 19 (Washington: GPO, 1901), p. 189. (Hereafter cited as *Senate Executive Journal.*)

[210] Jacobstein and Mersky, *The Rejected*, p. 86.

[211] *Senate Executive Journal*, vol. 19, p. 189.

[212] See, e.g., "The Chief Justiceship," *New York Tribune*, January 6, 1874, p. 1, which reported that the President "has at last discovered that the nomination of Mr. Williams to be Chief-Justice of the Supreme Court is not only a very unpopular one, but that his confirmation will be impossible...." See also Jacobstein and Mersky, *The Rejected*, pp. 84-86.

[213] *Senate Executive Journal,* vol. 19, p. 211.

[214] *Abraham, Justices, Presidents and Senators,* p. 147.

[215] *Thorpe, Appearance of Supreme Court Nominees,* p. 372.

[216] *Senate Executive Journal,* vol. 63, p. 293.

[217] *Thorpe, Appearance of Supreme Court Nominees,* pp. 372-373.

[218] Abraham, *Justices, Presidents and Senators*, p. 147.

[219] In October 8, 1991, floor remarks, Senate Majority Leader George J. Mitchell (D-ME) explained the need to delay the Thomas vote: "It is most unfortunate that we have been placed in this situation. But events which are unpredictable, unplanned, and unfortunate can and frequently do intervene and cause a change in the plans of human beings. That has now occurred in this matter, in my judgment.
"For that reason, I believe the action we have taken to change the time of the scheduled vote until next Tuesday [October 15], and to give time for further inquiry into this matter by the Judiciary Committee, is an appropriate action." Sen. George J. Mitchell, "Unanimous Consent Agreement," remarks in the Senate, *Congressional Record*, vol, 137, October 8, 1991, p. 25920.

[220] If, on the other hand, the Senate votes against confirmation, a resolution of disapproval is forwarded to the President.

[221] Sheldon Goldman, *Picking Federal Judges; Lower Court Selection form Roosevelt Through Reagan* (New Haven, CT: Yale University Press, 1997), p. 12.

[222] Sometimes, the swearing into office occurs before the new Justice actually receives the commission document. This, for instance, happened in 2005 with Chief Justice appointee John G. Roberts Jr. Immediately after President George W. Bush signed Roberts's commission, the new Chief Justice was sworn into office—receiving his commission document afterwards, when the Justice Department arranged for it to be hand-delivered to him at the Court.

[223] The Court itself regards the date a Justice takes the judicial oath as the beginning of his or her service, "for until that oath is taken he/she is not vested with the prerogatives of the office." Supreme Court, *Supreme Court of the United States*, p. 23.

[224] A news account noted the relatively recent advent of this pattern, when Justice Ruth Bader Ginsburg, on August 10, 1993, took her two oaths—the judicial oath, in private ceremony in the Court's conference room, and the constitutional oath, in a nationally televised ceremony in the White House's East Room. "Supreme Court appointees," the article observed, "always have taken both oaths, but only since 1986, when Ronald Reagan held a ceremony for the investiture of Associate Justice Antonin Scalia and Rehnquist, has the constitutional oath become part of a White House ceremony." Joan Biskupic, "Ginsburg Sworn In as 107th Justice and 2nd Woman on Supreme Court," *The Washington Post*, August 11, 1993, p. A6.
Each of the three persons appointed to the Court since Justice Ginsburg has taken the judicial oath in private (though each in a different setting) and the constitutional oath in public (all at the White House). The judicial oath was administered to Stephen G. Breyer in private in 1994 by Chief Justice William H. Rehnquist at the latter's vacation home in Greensboro, VT; to John G. Roberts Jr. in a private ceremony at the White House by Justice John Paul Stevens; and to Samuel A. Alito Jr. in private at the Supreme Court's conference room in 2006 by Chief Justice Roberts. On the same occasions that they took their judicial oaths in private, Roberts and Alito took their constitutional oaths as well—while, however, also taking their constitutional oaths a second time, in televised White House ceremonies.

[225] See, for example, Linda Greenhouse, "A Ceremonial Start to the Session as the Supreme Court Welcomes a New Chief Justice," *The New York Times*, October 4, 2005, p. 25.

[226] The most recently appointed Justice, Samuel A. Alito Jr., who initially took his judicial and constitutional oaths of office on January 31, 2006, had "already been on the job two weeks and been sworn in twice" before his investiture on the Court on February 16, 2006, at which he "joined colleagues in the courtroom for the first time." Gina Holland, Associated Press, "New Justice Samuel Alito Welcomed at Supreme Court," *San Diego Union-Tribune*, February 16, 2006 (accessed at http: //www. signonsandiego.com).

In: Supreme Court Appointment Process (Update) ISBN: 978-1-60876-934-6
Editors: Emilia S. Durand

Chapter 2

SUPREME COURT JUSTICES: DEMOGRAPHIC CHARACTERISTICS, PROFESSIONAL EXPERIENCE, AND LEGAL EDUCATION, 1789-2009*

Susan Navarro Smelcer

SUMMARY

On May 1, 2009, Justice David H. Souter announced his retirement as an Associate Justice when the U.S. Supreme Court recessed for the summer. To fill this vacancy, President Barack Obama selected Sonia Sotomayor, a judge from the U.S. Court of Appeals for the Second Circuit. In announcing the nomination, President Obama noted her Ivy League education and extensive judicial experience. President Obama also emphasized Sotomayor 's life story, discussing in particular her upbringing as a child of Puerto Rican-born parents in a Bronx housing project.

The Sotomayor nomination raised the prospect that, with her appointment, the nine-member Court would again have two female Justices and the first Justice to identify as Latina. The Sotomayor nomination also prompted renewed discussion among Senators, media commentators, and scholars regarding racial, ethnic, gender, religious, professional, and educational diversity on the Court. Against the backdrop of the Sotomayor nomination, this report examines the social, professional, and educational backgrounds of the Justices across the entire history of the Supreme Court.

Over time, the Supreme Court has become more diverse in some ways and more homogeneous in others. When first constituted, and throughout most of its history, no women or minorities served on the Court. This changed with the appointment of the first African-American Justice, Thurgood Marshall, in 1967, and the first female Justice, Sandra Day O'Connor, in 1981. When Justice Marshall retired from the Court in 1991, he was succeeded by another African-American, Justice Clarence Thomas. Although Justice O'Connor, upon her retirement in 2006, was succeeded by a male, Justice Samuel A. Alito Jr., the Court's membership once again, in August 2009, included two female Justices, upon the confirmation of Sonia Sotomayor.

The religious affiliations of the Court's members also has changed over time. For almost the first 50 years of the Court, all Justices were affiliated with protestant Christian churches. The first Jewish Justice, Louis Brandeis, was appointed in 1916. Currently, two Jewish Justices, Ruth Bader Ginsburg and Stephen G. Breyer, serve on the Court. The first Catholic Justice, Chief Justice Roger Brooke Taney, was appointed in 1836. With the confirmation of Justice Sotomayor, six of the nine current Justices identify as Roman Catholic.

The career experiences of the Court's Justices, while quite diverse in the past, have become more homogeneous in recent times. Historically, Justices had served in a variety of professions, such as in the Cabinet, in a federal or state legislative body, or in a private legal practice. In the last 50 years, however, Justices have more and more frequently been elevated from positions on the federal circuit courts of appeals. Of the nine current Justices, all possess federal circuit court experience, and six have served as government attorneys in some capacity. No sitting Justice has served in a federal or state Cabinet position or legislature. Justice Sonia Sotomayor brings both experience as a private practitioner and a government attorney and is the only current Justice on the Court to have experience as a federal trial judge.

Over time, Justices' legal educations have become more homogeneous, as well. In the last 20 years, especially, three Ivy League law schools—Harvard, Yale, and Columbia—have been disproportionately represented on the Court. Of the nine sitting Justices, eight have attended one of these three law schools,

* This is an edited, reformatted and augmented version of a CRS Report for Congress publication dated September 2009.

including recently confirmed Justice Sotomayor, who is a graduate of Yale Law School.

INTRODUCTION

On May 1, 2009, Justice David H. Souter announced his retirement as an Associate Justice when the U.S. Supreme Court recessed for the summer.[1] To fill the vacancy created by Justice Souter's resignation, President Barack Obama selected Sonia Sotomayor, a judge from the U.S. Court of Appeals for the Second Circuit. In announcing the nomination, the President noted her Ivy League education and extensive judicial experience, first as a federal trial judge and later as a federal appellate judge, as evidence of her qualifications to sit on the Court. President Obama also emphasized Judge Sotomayor's life story, discussing in particular her upbringing as a child of Puerto Rican-born parents in a Bronx housing project.[2]

The Constitution is silent on the qualifications necessary to be appointed to the Court. The only reference to the appointment of Justices in the U.S. Constitution occurs in Article II, Sec. 2, Cl. 1, which states that the President "shall nominate, and by and with the consent of the Senate, shall appoint ... Judges of the supreme Court." When selecting a Supreme Court nominee, Presidents have often been understood to consider, among other things, the demographic, professional, and educational backgrounds of potential nominees, as well as how their selection might affect the diversity of the Court's membership.[3] Presidents may choose a nominee with certain characteristics in part to satisfy particular constituencies. They may additionally perceive a nominee's demographic characteristics, professional experience, and legal education as important attributes for the next Supreme Court Justice to have.[4]

A White House news release, issued following President Obama's announcement of the Sotomayor nomination, emphasized the diversity of the nominee's prior professional experience. It noted that "[h]er American story and three decade career in nearly every aspect of the law provide Judge Sotomayor with unique qualifications to be the next Supreme Court Justice.... If confirmed, [she] would bring more federal judicial experience to the Supreme Court than any justice in 100 years, and more overall judicial experience than anyone confirmed for the Court in the past 70 years."[5]

Discussions regarding the importance and proper role of demographic characteristics in the selection of federal judges have occurred since the Carter Administration's concerted effort to appoint minorities and women to the federal bench.[6] As recently as Justice Sotomayor's confirmation hearings, Senators, the press, and others have debated the importance and appropriateness of achieving ethnic, gender, and other forms of diversity in an institution such as the Supreme Court.[7]

Beyond the effect of demographic characteristics such as race, ethnicity, gender, and religion, some scholars have examined whether a Justice's prior professional or educational experiences influence his or her decision making. Various academics have suggested that prior professional experience, such as prosecutorial experience;[8] previous service in federal, state, or local legislative, executive, or judicial positions;[9] and military service[10] may influence a Justice's perspective and decision-making process. In addition, scholars have hypothesized that a Justice's legal education may affect his or her decision making, as well.[11]

While a Justice's prior professional experience or legal education may influence his or her decision making, it has been suggested that the relative diversity of the Court with respect to demographic characteristics, professional experience, and legal education may also influence collegial, or group, decision making. In particular, it has been argued that the quality of the decisions made by a collective decision-making body, such as the Supreme Court, is dependent in part on the diversity of its membership.[12] Specifically, these scholars suggest that "the greater the diversity of participation by people of different backgrounds and experiences, the greater the range of ideas and information contributed to the [collective decision-making] process."[13]

Supreme Court Appointments in Historical Context

Historically, appointments to the Supreme Court have occurred against the backdrop of a continuing national debate about the role of the Court in our democratic system. In addition to considering a broad range of statutory and constitutional issues, the Court has addressed a wide range of disputes regarding statutory interpretation, policy questions, and the distribution of power in American society, including the balance of power between states and the federal government, the government and businesses, the government and individuals, and the three branches of the federal government.[14]

During roughly the first 60 years of the Republic's existence (1789-1850), issues regarding states' rights versus federal supremacy were often highly contentious. Throughout this period, presidential appointments to the Court reflected both the fragile political state of the union and an apparent desire of Presidents, in some cases, to use Supreme Court appointments to shift the balance of power in the direction of either the federal government or the states, depending on the philosophy of the Chief Executive. Presidents often appeared concerned with a nominee's state of residence, seeking balanced representation from each region of the country, or with a nominee's proven political loyalty or perceived political reliability once on the Court.[15]

Starting in the 1850s, as tensions over the appropriate division of power between the federal and state governments increased, Presidents appeared to seek different characteristics in their Supreme Court nominees. According to constitutional scholar and longtime observer of the Supreme Court, Henry J. Abraham, "mounting attacks on the Court because of what abolitionists termed its pro-Southern stance in slavery and fugitive slave issues" prompted Presidents, when making a nomination, to consider a nominee's perceived strength of character, among other attributes, to handle the difficult questions faced by the Court.[16] During and after the Civil War, until about 1880, Presidents sought Justices who could help ease tensions between the North and the South, who were geographically representative of the nation, and, in the case of Abraham Lincoln, who would further the President's interest in the war effort.[17]

In the 1880s, the national dialogue shifted to the implementation of laissez-faire economic policy and the ability of the government to regulate business practices; it could be argued that Presidents' criteria for selecting Supreme Court Justices also shifted to match these changing national priorities. This debate over the economic powers of the federal government continued well into the 20th century, culminating in President Franklin Delano Roosevelt's efforts to "pack the Court" with "New Deal" supporters in 1937. From 1881 through 1952, emphasis on a nominee's state of residence and prior judicial experience appeared generally, if not always, to wane. Instead, Presidents appeared to be chiefly influenced by considerations of political loyalty, personal relationships, and perceived reliability in the individuals' social and economic views in their selection of Supreme Court nominees. Arguably, this trend continued through the Truman Administration, where, Professor Abraham contends, all four of Truman's appointees were the result of "crony appointment[s]" and were good friends and political allies of the President.[18]

By the early 1 950s, however, the Court had begun its involvement in some of the most volatile social issues of the day, including cases involving the separation between church and state and racial discrimination. Upon the death of Chief Justice Frederick M. Vinson in 1953, President Dwight D. Eisenhower, according to Professor Abraham, looked outside of his circle of advisors and colleagues for someone who could command the respect of the nation and create geographic and religious balance on the Court.[19] Like Presidents before him, the newly elected President Eisenhower also desired a Chief Justice who would reflect his own "moderate progressivism, common sense, high ideals, and 'absence of extreme views.'"[20] His selection of Earl Warren as Chief Justice, however, resulted in what scholars describe as some of the Court's most controversial decisions, such as *Brown v. Board of Education* (1954),[21] *Abington School District v. Schempp* (1963),[22] and *Reynolds v. Sims* (1964).[23] Eisenhower, reportedly disappointed with his appointee's leadership on the Court, required that his next appointee have prior judicial experience so that he would have an "inkling of [the nominee's] philosophy."[24]

The nomination criteria of Eisenhower's successors, Presidents John F. Kennedy and Lyndon B. Johnson, marked a return, in the words of one scholar, to "the politics of patronage."[25] Kennedy and Johnson both purportedly rewarded personal loyalty in their nominations to the Court and encountered very little opposition in the Senate to their selections.[26] By the late 1 960s, however, the nomination process became highly contentious as a result of the "resentment against the [liberal jurisprudence of the] Supreme Court."[27] David Yalof, a scholar of the Supreme Court appointment process, explained the transition into a new era of politics in the following way:

> The battle over Abe Fortas's nomination [to the position of Chief Justice] in 1968 had ushered in a new and more contentious era for Supreme Court appointments. Divided government became a reality in the early 1970s, with Senators assuming an increasingly hostile posture against presidential nominees. Enhanced media attention of the process followed. Interest groups, including an increasingly aggressive professional bar [the American Bar Association], jockeyed for position to influence each vacancy.[28]

During the Nixon Administration, then assistant U.S. Attorney General and future Supreme Court Justice William Rehnquist advised Nixon's Attorney General that, while interest groups may object to a nominee's perceived policy positions, as indicated by prior deeds, past speeches, or judicial record, such objections "cannot successfully defeat a nominee" without some additional objection regarding the nominee's ethics or legal qualifications.[29]

As a result, it has been suggested, Presidents during this period more frequently sought nominees with impressive judicial qualifications. They purportedly did so not only to insulate a nominee from criticism, but also (as President Eisenhower had done) to gauge, from a nominee's judicial experience, how he or she might make decisions once on the Court.[30] Consistent with this hypothesis, the vast majority of Supreme Court Justices appointed in the last 30 years have had prior judicial experience, specifically experience as judges in the U.S. Courts of Appeals.

Over the course of two centuries, the importance of demographic characteristics, professional experience, and legal education in the selection of Justices has varied widely. This report examines these characteristics across the four historical periods described above (1789-1850, 1851-1880, 1881-1952, 1953-2009).[31] Specifically, the first section examines, for each of the time periods, the race, ethnicity, gender, and religious affiliation of the Justices. The second section examines the prior professional backgrounds of the Justices, including past experience in private practice or as government attorneys; as judges; as legislators or executives at the local, state, and federal level; and as members of the military. The third and final section examines the professional training and legal education of Supreme Court Justices, focusing on developments in legal education from 1789 to the present and the representation of Ivy League law schools on the Court.

Demographic Characteristics

Race and Ethnicity

Since the creation of the Court in 1789, its membership has largely reflected the class of white, land-owning males. Of the 111 men and women to serve on the Supreme Court, only 2 have self- identified as African-American. The first to join the Court, Justice Thurgood Marshall, was appointed by President Lyndon Johnson in 1967. Prior to his appointment, Marshall had worked as the director and counsel for the NAACP Legal Defense Fund for 21 years, served on the U.S. Court of Appeals for the Second Circuit for four years and, at the time of his appointment, was serving as the solicitor general of the United States. Hearings on Marshall's nomination lasted five days, longer than all but one other Supreme Court nominee to that point in time; Marshall was confirmed by a 69-11 vote.[32]

The second African-American to serve on the Court, Justice Clarence Thomas, was nominated by President George H.W. Bush to fill a vacancy created by Justice Marshall in 1991. At the time, Thomas was serving on the U.S. Court of Appeals for the District of Columbia and previously served as the director of the Equal Employment Opportunity Commission from 1982 through 1990. Thomas's confirmation hearings extended across 11 days. In the final 3 days of hearings, 21 public witnesses testified in response to accusations of sexual harassment, including Thomas himself. His nomination, reported without recommendation out of the Senate Judiciary Committee, was confirmed by a 52-48 vote.[33]

Until the confirmation of Justice Sonia Sotomayor, no Justice who identified as Hispanic or Latina had ever served on the Court.[34] However, as Sotomayor has explained, her identification as Latina is not reflective of a single idea or definitions of the term. In 2002, she noted,

> If I had pursued my career in my undergraduate history major, I would likely provide you with a very academic description of what being a Latino or Latina means. For example, I could define Latinos as those peoples and cultures populated or colonized by Spain who maintained or adopted Spanish or Spanish Creole as their language of communication. That antiseptic description however... does not explain why individuals like us, many of whom are born in this completely different American culture, still identify so strongly with those communities in which our parents were born and raised.[35]

Justice Sotomayor, born in New York to Puerto Rican-born parents, views the identification as embracing all of the language, food, and traditions of her family but without monolithically defining the term "Latina" as any one of those things. She recognizes that many people who identify as Latino or Latina may have had completely different cultural experiences.[36]

Gender

As with racial and ethnic minorities, women have been similarly unrepresented on the Court. In the 220-year history of the Court, only three women have served as Supreme Court Justices. The first, Sandra Day O'Connor, was appointed in 1981 by President Ronald Reagan, following a campaign promise that "[o]ne of the first Supreme Court vacancies in my administration will be filled with the most qualified woman I can find."[37] O'Connor, a former state legislator and state appellate court judge, was confirmed by a 99-0 vote in the Senate.

The second woman appointed to the bench, Ruth Bader Ginsburg, was appointed in 1993 by President William J. Clinton. A widely respected advocate of women's rights, Ginsburg was the first tenured female law professor at Columbia University, the first director of the American Civil Liberties Union's Women's Rights Project, and had successfully argued cases involving gender equality before the Court on five separate occasions. President Clinton purportedly gravitated toward Ginsburg due to former Solicitor General Erwin Griswold's comparison of her contribution to the advancement of women's rights through litigation to that of Justice Thurgood Marshall's contribution in the realm of civil rights.[38]

From the appointment of Justice Ginsburg in 1993 to the retirement of Justice O'Connor in 2005, two of the nine sitting Justices were women.[39] O'Connor's retirement reportedly prompted some political pressure on President George W. Bush that her replacement be a woman, including from First Lady Laura Bush.[40]

O'Connor herself hoped that President Bush would select a woman. Specifically, she noted, "It is important for the citizens of this country to see that in all areas of our governmental structures that women are also represented there."[41]

On July 19, 2005, 18 days after O'Connor's announcement, President Bush nominated John G. Roberts, Jr., a judge on the U.S. Court of Appeals for the District of Columbia, to be an Associate Justice. Upon the death of Chief Justice William H. Rehnquist, President Bush withdrew Roberts's nomination and, on the same day, nominated Roberts for the position of Chief Justice. To fill the vacancy created by O'Connor's retirement, President Bush nominated Harriet Miers, who was then serving in the position of White House counsel. Harriet Miers's nomination was withdrawn 52 days later, and the name of Samuel A. Alito, Jr., was submitted in her place.[42]

Another vacancy would not occur again until the retirement of Justice David Souter in June 2009. Confirmed on August 6, 2009, Sonia Sotomayor joined Justice Ginsburg on the bench as the third woman to be appointed to the Court.

Religion

Religious diversification on the Court began to occur long before the inclusion of minorities and women on the Court. Figure 1 displays the distribution of the religious affiliation of Supreme Court Justices appointed during each of the four periods of the Court's history, as discussed above. As illustrated in Figure 1, the first Justices were almost exclusively affiliated with protestant Christian churches. In the first 60 years of the Court, 30 there were (96.8%) of the 31 Justices appointed that were protestant Christians. Seventeen (54.8%) of the 31 were Episcopalian,[43] and the 13 (41.9%) were of other Protestant denominations, such as, Congregationalism, Methodism, and Presbyterianism.

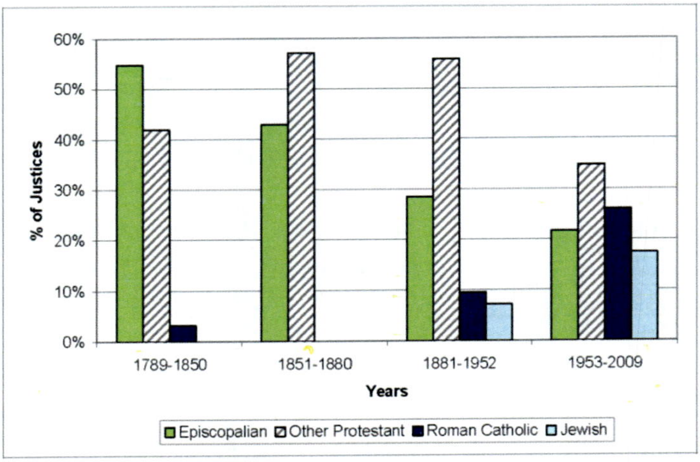

Source: Lee Epstein, Jeffrey A. Segal, Harold J. Spaeth, and Thomas G. Walker, *Supreme Court Compendium: Data, Decisions, and Developments*, 4th ed. (Washington, DC: CQ Press, 2007).

Figure 1. Religious Affiliation of Supreme Court Justices, By Appointment Date, 1789-2009

The lone non-Protestant Christian Justice appointed during this period and the Court's first Roman Catholic was Chief Justice Roger B. Taney, who was appointed by Andrew Jackson in 1836. The second Roman Catholic Justice, Edward Douglass White, was not appointed until 1894. Since White's appointment, however, the number of Roman Catholic Justices on the Court has steadily increased. Between 1881 and 1952, 4 (9.5%) of the 42 Justices appointed were Roman Catholic.[44] Between 1953 and the present, 7 (29.2%) of the 24 Justices appointed have been Roman Catholic. When Samuel Alito, a Roman Catholic, joined the Court in 2006 to replace Justice Sandra Day O'Connor, an Episcopalian, a majority of the Court's membership was Roman Catholic for the first time in the nation's history. This Roman Catholic majority grew from 5 to 6 justices with the confirmation of Justice Sotomayor.

Although the first Roman Catholic Justice was appointed to the Court in 1836, the first Jewish Justice did not join the Court until 1916, with President Woodrow Wilson's appointment of Louis Brandeis. Brandeis was branded as a "radical" due to his socially conscious legal work and was the target of anti-Semitic forces.[45] Although Brandeis neither appeared at nor commented on the proceedings, the Senate Judiciary devoted 19 days of hearings to the nomination—the longest of any of Supreme Court nominee.[46]

The next Jewish members of the Court were not appointed until the 193 0s, with the appointment of Justices Benjamin Cardozo in 1932 to replace Oliver Wendell Holmes, and Felix Frankfurter in 1939 to replace Cardozo upon his untimely death.[47] Unlike Justice Brandeis, Justices Cardozo and Frankfurter received less contentious and, as a result, much shorter confirmation hearings. Cardozo's 1932 confirmation process lasted only nine days from Senate receipt of the nomination to confirmation by unanimous voice vote.[48] Only one of those days was dedicated to a hearing before the Senate Judiciary Committee. Like Brandeis, Cardozo chose not to appear before the committee.[49] The process of appointing Justice Frankfurter took 33% longer (12, as compared with 9, days) and included 3 days of public hearings before his eventual confirmation, also by voice vote on the floor of the Senate. Unlike Brandeis and Cardozo, Frankfurter chose to testify before the Senate Judiciary Committee.[50]

Since the 1930s, however, public hearings have become standard practice, and nominees, regardless of the level of controversy surrounding their nomination, routinely appear before the Judiciary Committee.[51] The nominations of the two Jewish Justices currently serving on the Court, Stephen Breyer and Ruth Bader Ginsburg, were subject to four days of public hearings each.[52] Both attended those hearings.

PROFESSIONAL BACKGROUND

The men and women appointed to the Supreme Court have held a variety of professional backgrounds. While 64% of all Justices appointed to the Court have had some form of judicial experience, Justices have also held positions in federal, state, and local governments, and in the private sector. Those positions have ranged from legislator, to professional athlete,[53] to President of the United States.

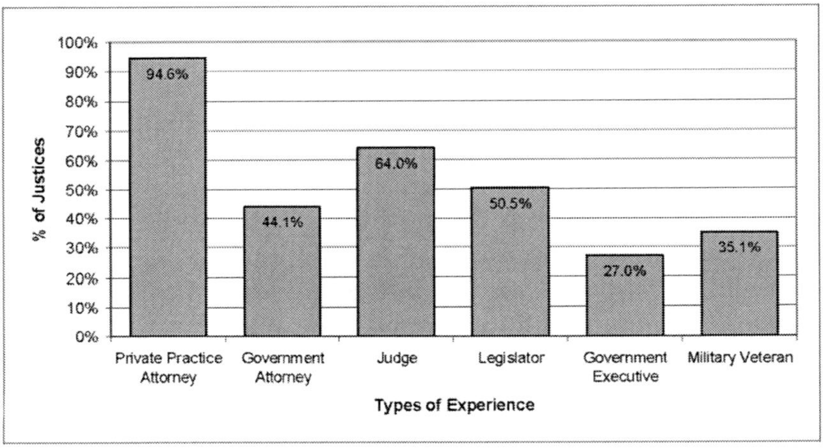

Source: CRS analysis of data from the Federal Judicial Center's *Federal Judicial Biographical Database (*www.fjc.gov) and Lee Epstein, Jeffrey A. Segal, Harold J. Spaeth, and Thomas G. Walker, *Supreme Court Compendium: Data, Decisions, and Developments*, 4th ed. (Washington, DC: CQ Press, 2007).

Figure 2. Prior Experience of Supreme Court Justices. Chief Justices and Associate Justices, 1789-2009

Overwhelmingly, Supreme Court Justices come to the bench with some form of non-judicial legal experience. As illustrated in Figure 2, 105 (94.6%) of the 111 Justices appointed to the Supreme Court have engaged in private practice, although only 49 (44.1%) had served as an attorney for a federal, state, or local entity. Across its history, 71 (64.0%) Justices came to the Supreme Court with prior judicial experience in a lower federal or state court. A smaller number of Justices (56 or 50.5%) have come to the bench with prior legislative experience and fewer (30 or 27.0%) have possessed executive experience. While experience in private practice and prior judicial experience have been the most common employment patterns among Supreme Court Justices, 39 (35.1%) have also served in the military.

Experience in Private Practice

As indicated in Figure 3, the vast majority of Court appointees have spent some time in private practice. From 1789-1850, all but two Supreme Court Justices had been employed in private practice.[54] From 1851-1952, all 56 appointees to the Court were engaged in private practice at some point in their careers. In the past 56 years, only four (16.7%) of the 24 Justices had never worked for a private law firm. Justice Clarence Thomas was the first in 180 years to possess no experience in private practice.

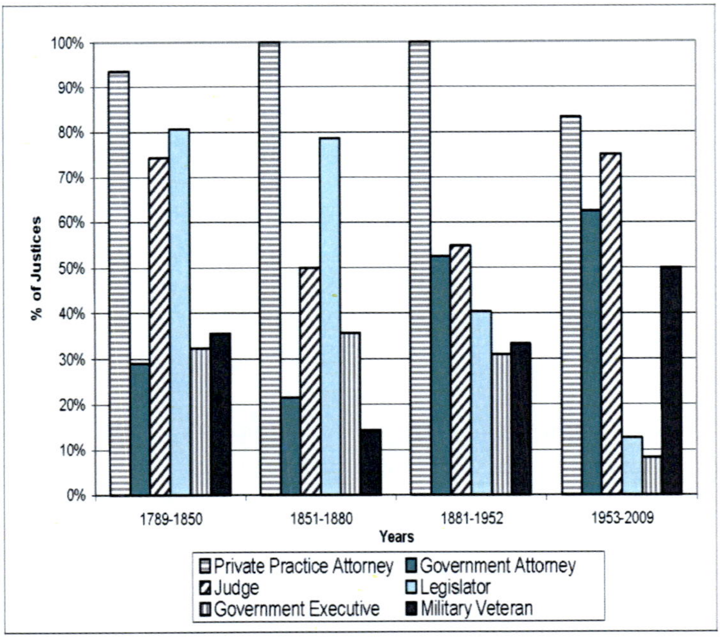

Source: **CRS analysis of data from the Federal Judicial Center's** *Federal Judicial Biographical Database (*www.fjc.gov) and Lee Epstein, Jeffrey A. Segal, Harold J. Spaeth, and Thomas G. Walker, *Supreme Court Compendium: Data, Decisions, and Developments*, 4th ed. (Washington, DC: CQ Press, 2007).

Figure 3. Prior Occupations of Supreme Court Justices Over Time By Appointment Date and Type of Experience, 1789-2009

Notably, like Justice Thomas, three of the next four appointees—Ginsburg, Breyer, and Alito—also lacked experience in private practice. In contrast, the most recent appointee, Sonia Sotomayor, spent eight years in private practice at the firm of Parvia & Harcourt in New York, which places her experience in line with that of the vast majority of Supreme Court Justices.

Experience as a Government Attorney

Of the 111 individuals appointed to the Supreme Court since 1789, 49 (44.1%) have served as government attorneys. This category is a broad one and encompasses any position in which the Justice may have served as a counsel or attorney for a local, state, or federal agency or institution. For example, included in this category are Justice Hugo Black, who worked as a prosecuting attorney in Birmingham, Alabama, from 1914 through 1917; Justice Thurgood Marshall, who served as the solicitor general of the United States from 1965-1967; Chief Justice Oliver Ellsworth, who served as a state attorney in Hartford County, Connecticut, from 1777-1785; and Justice Stephen G. Breyer, who served as an assistant special prosecutor on the Watergate Special Prosecution Force in 1973 and a special counsel for the Administrative Practices Subcommittee of the U.S. Senate Judiciary Committee from 1974-1975.

Justices with experience as United States attorneys are also included in this category.[55] Of the 49 Justices who worked as government attorneys, only four were U.S. attorneys. The first U.S. attorney to join the Court was Noah Swayne, appointed in 1862; the second and third were Stanley Matthews and William Moody, in 1881 and 1906. The most recently appointed former U.S. attorney, Samuel Alito, was confirmed in 2006.

Of the 31 individuals appointed to the Court between 1789 and 1850, 9 (23.0%) had prior experience as government attorneys. Of these 9, 5 served as the attorney general for their respective states for at least one year,[56] 3 served as state district attorneys,[57] and 1—Chief Justice Roger B. Taney—served as the Attorney General of the United States. The number of Supreme Court Justices with this type of experience decreased slightly between 1851 and 1880. Of the 14 individuals appointed during this period, 3 (21.4%) had worked as government attorneys. Two of these Justices served as attorney generals of their respective states, one of whom also served as the Attorney General of the United States.[58] The remaining Justice served as both a county prosecutor and a U.S. attorney prior to joining the Court.[59]

Since 1851, the percentage of Justices with experience as government attorneys has increased dramatically, rising from 21.4% of the Justices appointed between 1851 and 1880 to 62.5% of the Justices appointed since 1953. Of the 42 Justices appointed from 1881 through 1952, 22 (52.4%) served as government attorneys at some point in their careers. Of these 22, 15 (68.2%) held multiple positions as government attorneys at local, state, and federal levels of government. For example, Justice Stanley Matthews served as both the assistant prosecutor of Hamilton County, Ohio (1845), and U.S. attorney for the Southern District of Ohio (1858-1861). Justice Joseph McKenna was a district attorney in Solano County, California (1866-1870), and the Attorney General of the United States (1897).

Since 1953, 15 of the 24 appointees (62.5%) came to the bench with prior experience as government attorneys. As in the previous period, a majority of these Justices held multiple positions as government attorneys. Of the 15 appointed with such experience, 8 (53.3%) held multiple positions. Chief Justice Earl Warren, for example, held five different prosecutorial positions, including that of city attorney for Oakland, California; district attorney for Alameda County, California; and attorney general for the state of California.

Six of the nine members of the current Court also served as government attorneys. In addition to serving as a U.S. attorney, Justice Samuel Alito worked as an assistant U.S. attorney and in the offices of the Attorney General and solicitor general. Like Justice Alito, Chief Justice John Roberts also served in a variety of government attorney positions, most notably as an associate counsel to President Ronald Reagan in the White House Counsel's Office. Justice Stephen Breyer, in addition to the service described above, was a special assistant to the assistant U.S. attorney general for antitrust and the chief counsel to the U.S. Senate Judiciary Committee. Justice Clarence Thomas spent time as assistant attorney general for the state of Missouri from 1974 through 1977. Justice Antonin Scalia worked as an assistant attorney general in the U.S. Department of Justice Office of Legal Counsel from 1974 through 1977. Recently appointed Justice Sonia Sotomayor was an assistant district attorney in the New York County District Attorney's Office under Robert Morgenthau from 1979 through 1984.

Judicial Experience

While prior judicial experience has been an important factor in the modern confirmation process, presidential emphasis on such experience in the selection of Justices has varied over the history of the Court.[60] Preference for judicial experience, whether state or federal, can be explained in part by the changing character of the federal judiciary. Congress created the basic organizational structure of the federal judiciary—a structure that still exists to this day—with the Judiciary Act of 1789. The Judiciary Act divided the new nation into 13 districts, for which district court judgeships were created. District courts held original jurisdiction over admiralty and maritime cases, as well as some minor civil and criminal cases. The appointed district court judge sat with a Supreme Court Justice to constitute the circuit court for the district.[61] Circuit courts served as trial courts for "most criminal cases, for suits between citizens of different states (diversity cases), and for civil suits initiated by the United States." Circuit courts also "exercised appellate jurisdiction over all but the smallest admiralty cases and other civil suits that originated in the U.S. district courts."[62] In order to exercise this appellate jurisdiction, however, a Supreme Court Justice was required to preside over the proceedings.

In a time of poor roads, slow transportation, and rampant disease, "riding circuit," or traveling from the nation's capital to districts to hold circuit court, was an extreme hardship for Supreme Court Justices.[63] For example, Justice James Wilson died in 1798 after contracting malaria while riding circuit.[64] These hardships and an increase in the federal caseload led Congress to reform the circuit courts. In 1869, Congress created separate circuit court judgeships for each of the circuits. These new judges, unlike the district court judges operating in the circuit, were authorized to conduct appellate business, with the district court judge, in the absence of a Supreme Court Justice. The circuit courts were stripped of their appellate jurisdiction with the creation of the modern Courts of Appeals in 1891 and eventually abolished in January of 1912.[65]

It is unsurprising, then, that few Supreme Court Justices appointed between 1789 and 1850 possessed district court experience and none possessed circuit court experience. Justices appointed during this period did, however, possess extensive state judicial experience. Twenty- two (71.0%) of the 31 Justices appointed during this period, as illustrated in Figure 4, served on a colonial or state court, whereas only 3 (9.7%) served on a federal district court and 8 (25.8%) lacked judicial experience entirely. Between 1789 and 1850, the percentage of sitting Justices with state judicial experience, for all but three years,[66] never dropped below 5 0.0%, as indicated in Figure 5. Usually, it was much higher. Justices' state court experience was, in many cases, quite extensive. The most experienced, William Cushing, served as a judge in one capacity or another in Massachusetts for 29 years, from 1760 to

1789, at which time he was appointed to the Supreme Court. Only 8 (25.8%) of the Justices appointed during this period possessed no judicial experience.

While circuit courts have existed since the Judiciary Act of 1789, separate circuit court judgeships were not created until 1869. The modern courts of appeals were created by the Judiciary Act of 1891, commonly known as the Evarts Act. Thus, the dashed line representing the percentage of sitting Justices with circuit court experience does not begin until 1869. The solid vertical line (placed at 1891) indicates the creation date of modern circuit courts of appeals.

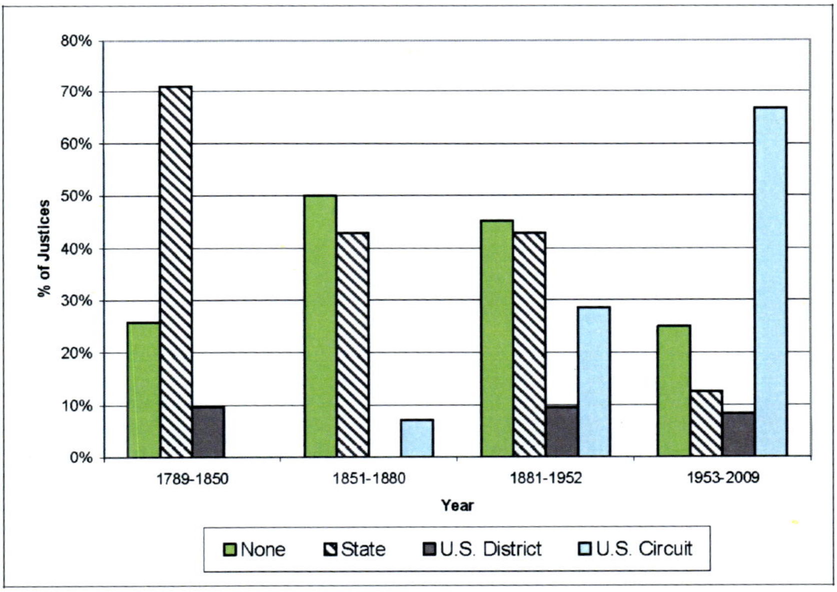

Source: **CRS analysis of data from the Federal Judicial Center's** *Federal Judicial Biographical Database (*www.fjc.gov) and Lee Epstein, Jeffrey A. Segal, Harold J. Spaeth, and Thomas G. Walker, *Supreme Court Compendium: Data, Decisions, and Developments*, 4th ed. (Washington, DC: CQ Press, 2007).

Notes: Separate circuit court judgeships were first created by the Judiciary Act of 1801 but abolished 13 months later with the Judiciary Act of 1802. Separate circuit court judgeships were not again created until 1869, when a single circuit court judgeship was created in each of the geographical circuits. As a result, no judge could have been a circuit court judge before 1869, precluding the elevation of a judge with such experience before that time.

Figure 4. Percentage of Total Justices Appointed with Judicial Experience By Appointment Date and Type of Experience, 1789-2009

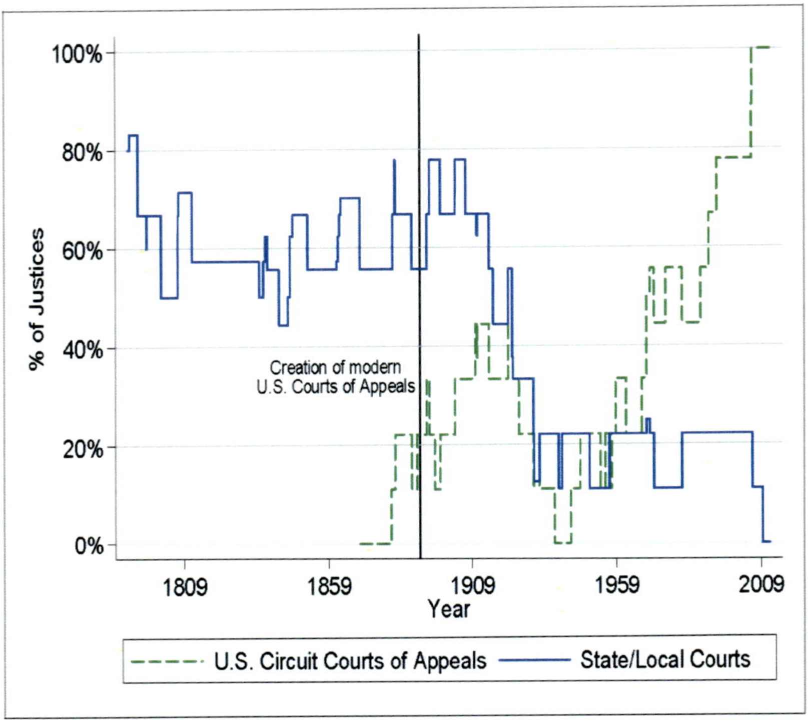

Source: **CRS analysis of data from the Federal Judicial Center's** *Federal Judicial Biographical Database (*www.fjc.gov) and Lee Epstein, Jeffrey A. Segal, Harold J. Spaeth, and Thomas G. Walker, *Supreme Court Compendium: Data, Decisions, and Developments*, ^{4th} ed. (Washington, DC: CQ Press, 2007).

Notes: This graph displays the percentage of sitting Justices with either state court or circuit court experience. Unlike Figure 4, this graph displays the percentage of Justices serving on the Court at any particular time in history. For example, in 2007, the graph indicates that 11.1% of sitting Justices (one of nine) possessed state court experience, and 100.0% (nine of nine) possessed circuit court experience.

While circuit courts have existed since the Judiciary Act of 1789, separate circuit court judgeships were not created until 1869. The modern courts of appeals were created by the Judiciary Act of 1891, commonly known as the Evarts Act. Thus, the dashed line representing the percentage of sitting Justices with circuit court experience does not begin until 1869. The solid vertical line (placed at 1891) indicates the creation date of modern circuit courts of appeals.

Figure 5. Percentage of Sitting Justices with Prior Judicial Experience By Type of Experience, 1789-2009

From 1851 through 1880, only one appointee had served on a U.S. circuit court and none on a U.S. district court. As in the previous period, Justices accrued judicial experience at the state, as opposed to the federal, level. Of the 14 Justices appointed during this period, 6 (42.8%) were formerly state court judges, although only one was elevated directly from that position.[67] During this time, no fewer than 50.0%, and as many as 70.0%, of sitting Justices possessed state court experience, as illustrated in Figure 5.

Despite the continued appointment of Justices with state court experience between 1851 and 1880, Presidents appeared to emphasize characteristics other than judicial experience in choosing nominees. Appointees were selected, in part, because they were perceived as capable of maintaining public respect for the Court in an increasingly hostile political environment and, in many cases, had demonstrated personal loyalty to the President. Most importantly, Presidents sought appointees supportive of the Administration's agenda with respect to the growing sectional tensions prior to the Civil War, during the conflict, and through the traumatic reconstruction process that followed.[68] Changes such as these in Presidents' selection criteria may explain why only 50.0% of Justices appointed between 1851 and 1880 possessed state or federal judicial experience, as compared with 74.2% in the previous period.

President Millard Fillmore's selection of Benjamin R. Curtis in 1851 illustrates this shift. Curtis, who lacked state and federal judicial experience, possessed characteristics Fillmore perceived to be more important in the difficult political climate of the 1 850s, such as "strength of character, and the potential for judicial presence [as well as] an understanding of contemporary history and politics." Fillmore additionally required that his nominee be a "Whig, a comparatively young man, and a New Englander."[69] One scholar noted that, for President Abraham Lincoln, "the effect a proposed member might have on the conduct of the [Civil War] was of paramount importance. All other considerations were secondary," including prior judicial experience.[70]

Between 1881 and 1952, appointees with state court experience declined slightly from 42.8% in the previous period to 40.5%. Conversely, appointees with federal court experience increased substantially. Four (9.5%) of the 42 Justices appointed possessed federal district court experience, and 11 (26.2%) possessed federal circuit court experience. One Justice, Samuel Blatchford, appointed by President Chester Arthur in 1882, possessed both district and circuit court experience.

Presidents during this period, however, did not uniformly consider judicial experience as necessary for appointment to the Court, which may explain why

19 (42.5%) of the 42 appointees lacked lower federal or state court experience. While the first President in this period, Chester Arthur, appeared to consider such experience important,[71] his successor, President Grover Cleveland, the first Democrat elected to the presidency since 1860, did not. Cleveland sought nominees who, like himself, were "Democrat[s] in good standing," were "known to him personally," shared his policy preferences, and hailed from "an appropriate geographic area."[72] Although Cleveland did not appear to place importance on prior judicial experience, two of his four appointees to the Court did serve as lower court judges. Of the two, only one, Rufus Peckham of New York, was elevated from a state court. The other, Edward Douglass White, was a sitting U.S. Senator at the time of his appointment.

Unlike his predecessor, the selection criteria of President Benjamin Harrison emphasized not only that the appointee should possess similar policy preferences and party affiliation as the President, but also that nominees should be "experienced practicing lawyers and judges."[73] All but one of Harrison's four appointees possessed judicial experience. The next two Presidents, William McKinley and Theodore Roosevelt, deemphasized judicial experience in their selection criteria, although Roosevelt delineated "competence" an important criterion. Roosevelt was the first President to "go on public record with a policy of downgrading geography" as an important consideration in the selection of Supreme Court Justices.[74]

President William H. Taft, who would later serve as the Court's Chief Justice, explicitly emphasized judicial experience,[75] with five of six appointees possessing either state or federal experience or both. President Woodrow Wilson, Taft's successor, deemphasized judicial experience as a selection criterion and selected Supreme Court Justices who were personal or professional acquaintances and who possessed similar political opinions.[76]

Presidents who followed Wilson continued this trend. Only half of Warren G. Harding's appointees possessed any form of judicial experience, and Calvin Coolidge's lone appointee, Harlan Fiske Stone, had no judicial experience. Of Franklin D. Roosevelt's eight Associate Justice appointees, only three had any form of judicial experience and, of these, just one served on the federal bench.[77] Only one of President Harry Truman's three Associate Justice appointees possessed judicial experience.[78]

Both Roosevelt and Truman, however, chose Chief Justices with federal judicial experience, although such considerations, reportedly, were not important in their selections of Associate Justices. Roosevelt chose to elevate Harlan Fiske Stone, who, while not having any lower court experience, had served on the Supreme Court for over 16 years before his elevation. Truman appointed Frederick M. Vinson, who had served for almost six years on the U.S. Court of Appeals for the District of Columbia, to the position after Chief Justice Stone's death in 1946.[79]

Although Presidents increasingly selected appointees with federal judicial experience during this period, the Justices' length of tenure on lower federal courts varied widely. Most Justices possessed less than 10 years of federal judicial service, with 10 of the 14 Justices having served between 2.0 to 8.4 years in the federal district or circuit courts. A smaller number possessed well above 10 years of service, with four Justices having served between 14.7 and 16.7 years before their elevation to the Court. Of these four, one served entirely on a circuit court, two on district courts, and one on both district and circuit courts.

Since 1953, most Presidents have tended to emphasize the importance of judicial experience, especially in the federal circuit courts. Immediately prior to President Dwight D. Eisenhower's appointment of Chief Justice Earl Warren in 1953, only one of nine sitting Justices possessed state court experience and two possessed circuit court experience; none had served on a federal district court (see Figure 5). Following Warren's appointment, however, the Court began to consider more cases that were widely publicized and had widespread, controversial social consequences, contrary to Eisenhower's reported desire that the Chief Justice reflect his own "moderate progressivism, common sense, high ideals, and 'absence of extreme views.'" Due to his disappointment with Warren's leadership, however, Eisenhower required that his next appointee have prior judicial experience so that he would have an "inkling of [the nominee's] philosophy."[80]

Presidents John F. Kennedy and Lyndon B. Johnson, unlike Eisenhower, purportedly rewarded personal loyalty in their nominations to the Court; judicial experience was not required.[81] Such "patronage" appointment encountered very little opposition in the Senate in the early and mid- 1960s.[82] By the late 1960s, however, the confirmation process had become very contentious due to "resentment against the [liberal jurisprudence of the] Supreme Court,"[83] and patronage appointments, such as Johnson's nomination of his close friend and sitting Associate Justice Abe Fortas to Chief Justice, began to encounter heavy opposition in the Senate.[84]

Presidents following Johnson, as a result, began to consistently favor nominees with prior judicial experience, especially those with service in the federal circuit courts, in order to both better predict nominees' behavior once confirmed[85] and avoid criticism in the press and opposition in the Senate.[86] Such experience has increasingly become an almost standard background feature of every Supreme Court nominee. As one scholar noted, "[F]ederal circuit court judges have become the 'darlings' of the selection process."[87] Of the 24 Justices appointed since 1953, 16 (66.7%) of the 24 Justices served on a federal circuit court, 2 of whom also served on federal district courts[88] and 1 on a state court.[89] Only 3 (8.3%) of the 24 appointed during this period possessed state court experience. Whereas in 1953 only one sitting Justice possessed federal circuit court experience, all nine current Justices have such experience (see Figure 5).[90]

Most Justices appointed since 1953 possessed less than 10 years of federal judicial experience, although the range and minimum length of tenure is shorter than in the previous period. Nine of the 16 Justices appointed since 1953 served between 0.5 and 5.2 years on lower federal courts before their elevation, as compared with 2.0 to 8.4 years in the previous period. Seven of the 16 Justices served for more than 10 years on the lower federal court, with tenures ranging between 10.7 and 17.0 years. Four of the last five appointees each served as federal judges for more than 13 years before their elevation to the Court.

The most recent appointee, Sonia Sotomayor, possesses more federal lower court experience than any Justice in American history.[91] In announcing her nomination, President Obama emphasized Sonia Sotomayor's qualifications as a former U.S. district court judge and current U.S. circuit court judge. The President explained, "Over a distinguished career that spans three decades, Judge Sotomayor has worked at almost every level of our judicial system, providing her with a depth of experience and a breadth of perspective that will be invaluable as a Supreme Court justice." The President continued by stressing that "[w]alking in the door, she would bring more experience on the bench and more varied experience on the bench than anyone currently serving on the United States Supreme Court had when they were appointed."[92]

Prior Political Experience

Legislative experience

Legislative experience among Supreme Court Justices has exhibited a consistent decline since the middle of the 19th century. Prior to 1850, the appointment of Justices with legislative experience at the federal, state, or local level was not uncommon. From 1789-1850, 25 (80.6%) of the 31 Justices appointed had some form of legislative experience. Twenty-four Justices

(77.4%) had served in a state or colonial legislative body, 6 (19.4%) in the Continental Congress, 3 (25.8%) were previously U.S. Senators, and 8 (6.3%) were previously Members of the U.S. House of Representatives.

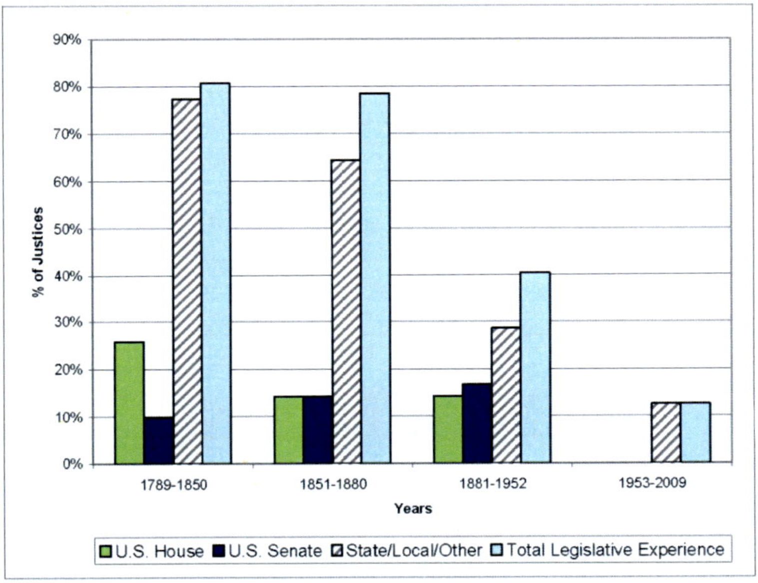

Source: CRS analysis of data from the Federal Judicial Center's *Federal Judicial Biographical Database* (www.fjc.gov).

Notes: The category "State/Local/Other" also includes service in the Continental Congress. In most cases, if a Justice has served as a delegate to the Continental Congress, he has also served as a member of a colonial or state legislature. Justice James Wilson, the fourth Justice appointed by Washington, served in the Continental Congress but no other state legislative body.

Figure 6. Legislative Experience over Time
By Appointment Date and Type of Experience, 1789-2009

When choosing nominees for the Supreme Court, President George Washington desired, among other things, that his nominees be politically involved in their local communities and home states and sought nominees with both judicial and legislative experience.[93] Of the 10 appointments made by Washington, 9 had prior legislative experience. Like Washington, his successor, President John Adams, reportedly viewed public service as an important qualification for a Justice. Two of his three appointees, including

Chief Justice John Marshall, possessed either state or federal legislative experience.[94]

However, while President Washington was purported to have valued both state political service and prior judicial experience as distinct qualifications, some later Presidents appeared not to distinguish between the two when considering potential nominees for the Court. For example, James Monroe was reported to have viewed judicial experience as interchangeable with "other high public-service experience," such as executive or legislative experience, when determining the qualifications of nominees.[95] Similarly, President Andrew Jackson was reported to have valued public service, but he did not emphasize judicial experience as a separate qualification from legislative experience.[96]

After 1850, however, the percentage of Supreme Court Justices with legislative experience began to decline. Between 1851 and 1880, 11 (78.6%) of the 14 Justices appointed had some form of prior legislative experience. In particular, nine (64.3%) had served in their state's legislature or another local legislative body, two (14.3%) in the U.S. House of Representatives, and two (14.3%) as U.S. Senators.

Whereas 71.4% of Justices appointed between 1850 and 1881 held some form of legislative position, only 40.5% (17 of 42) Justices appointed between 1881 and 1952 had similar legislative experience. Six (14.3%) had served as Members of the U.S. House of Representatives, 7 (16.7%) as U.S. Senators, and 12 (28.6%) as legislators in state or local legislative bodies.

Since 1953, only 3 (12.5%) of the 24 Justices appointed possessed any form of legislative experience, and none served as Members of the U.S. House of Representatives or U.S. Senate. One of these two Justices, Lewis Powell, served as chairman of the Richmond Public School Board from 1952 through 1961. Another, Potter Stewart, served on the Cincinnati, Ohio, city council from 1950 through 1953. The third, Sandra Day O'Connor, served in the Arizona Senate from 1969 through 1975. Following this trend, President Obama's appointee to the Court, Justice Sonia Sotomayor, has no prior legislative experience.

Executive experience

Table 1 lists four types of executive experience Supreme Court Justices have possessed when appointed to the Supreme Court: experience as a mayor, governor or lieutenant governor, presidential appointee, and U.S. President. Some Justices have served in more than one of these positions. For example, Chief Justice William Howard Taft served as the civil governor of the

Philippine Islands, Secretary of War, and President of the United States before being appointed Chief Justice by President Warren G. Harding in 1921.

Table 1. Executive Experience of Supreme Court Justices by Appointment Date and Type of Experience from 1789-2009

	Mayors	Governors/ Lt Governors	Presidential Appointees	U.S. Presidents	Total Executive
1789- 1850 (*N*=31)	1 (3.2%)	5 (16.1%)	8 (25.0%)	—	12(38.7%)
1851-1880 (*N*= 14)	2 (14.3%)	2 (14.3%)	5 (35.7%)	—	8 (57.1%)
1881-1952 (*N*=42)	—	4(9.5%)	16 (38.1%)	1 (2.3%)a	16 (38.1%)
1953-2009 (*N*=24)	—	1 (4.2%)	7 (29.2%)	—	8 (33.3%)
Total (*N*=1 11)	3 (2.7%)	12 (10.8%)	36 (32.4%)	1 (0.9%)	44 (39.6%)

Source: CRS analysis of data from the Federal Judicial Center's *Federal Judicial Biographical Database (*www.fjc.gov) and Lee Epstein, Jeffrey A. Segal, Harold J. Spaeth, and Thomas G. Walker, *Supreme Court Compendium: Data, Decisions, and Developments*, 4th ed. (Washington, DC: CQ Press, 2007).

Notes: The percentages listed in each row indicate the percentage of Justices appointed in that period who possessed the characteristic of interest. "N" indicates the number of Justices appointed during each time period.

a. William Howard Taft, the 27th President of the United States, is the only former President to be appointed to the Court.

Between 1789 and 1952, more than 40% of the Justices appointed to the Court possessed some form of executive experience. Across this 163-year period, 11 governors or lieutenant governors and 29 former presidential appointees were appointed to the Court.[97] As with legislative experience, however, a smaller number of nominees with executive experience were appointed to the Court in the last 56 years. One Justice, Earl Warren, served as governor of California prior to his 1953 appointment as Chief Justice by Dwight D. Eisenhower in 1953. Another, Arthur Goldberg, served as Secretary of Labor when appointed to the Court by John F. Kennedy in 1962. The other six Justices held positions such as United States attorney, chairman of the Administrative Office of United States, and chairman of the Equal Employment Opportunity Commission.

Prior Military Experience

The number of Supreme Court Justices with military experience has fluctuated over time, and military service patterns of Justices reflect the history of American military engagement at home and abroad. Since 1789, the United States has engaged in five declared wars with foreign nations, the Civil War, and prior to this time period, the Revolutionary War.[98]

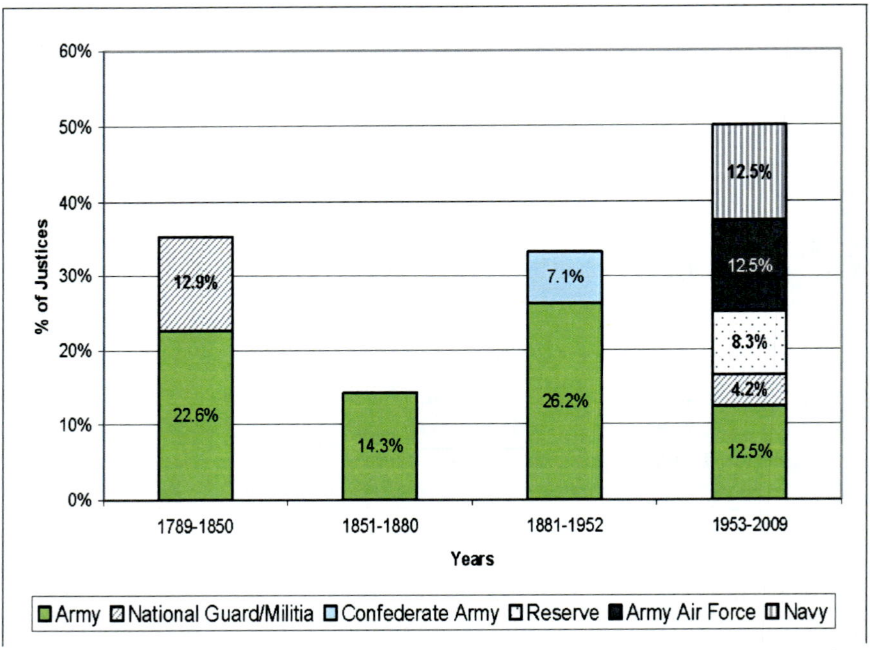

Source: CRS analysis of data from the Federal Judicial Center's *Federal Judicial Biographical Database (*www.fjc.gov) and Lee Epstein, Jeffrey A. Segal, Harold J. Spaeth, and Thomas G. Walker, *Supreme Court Compendium: Data, Decisions, and Developments*, 4th ed. (Washington, DC: CQ Press, 2007).

Notes: Categories of service have been simplified for the purposes of display. For example, the category "Army" includes service in the Continental Army (which is a distinct body of the Army that formed after the Revolutionary War) and the Union Army. In particular, between 1881 and 1952, three of the nine Justices who are categorized as serving in the Army had served in the Union Army during the Civil War.

Figure 7. Military Service of Supreme Court Justices By Appointment Date and Type of Experience, 1789-2009

Prior to 1851, more than 35% of the Supreme Court appointees possessed military experience, including the first Chief Justice of the Supreme Court, John Jay, and the longest serving Chief Justice, John Marshall. The military experience of the Justices appointed during this time was derived almost exclusively from service in the Continental Army or local or state militias during the Revolutionary War.[99] The two Justices appointed during this period who did not serve in the Revolutionary War fought in the War of 1812.[100]

Only 2 of the 18 Justices (14.3%) appointed between 1851 and 1880 possessed military experience, as opposed to 9 of the 31 Justices (35.5%) appointed prior to 1851. Both of these Justices, John Marshall Harlan I and William B. Woods, served in the Union Army during the Civil War and were appointed by President Rutherford B. Hayes.[101]

Presidents continued to appoint Justices to the Court who had fought in the Civil War between 1881 and 1952. Between 1881 and 1900, Presidents appointed five Justices who fought in the Civil War, with two having served in the Confederate Army.[102] Later in this period, Presidents appointed nine World War I veterans.[103] In total, 14 (33.3%) of the 42 Justices appointed possessed military experience.

Since 1953, the percentage of Justices with military experience increased to 50.0%, with 12 of 24 Justices having some form of military experience. Unlike Justices in previous periods, however, more recently appointed Justices have served during periods of both war and peace. Eight of the 12 Justices with military experience fought in World War II (two in the Army, four in the Army Air Force,[104] and three in the Navy). John Paul Stevens, who served as a lieutenant commander in the U.S. Navy from 1942 through 1945, is the only current Justice to have served during wartime.

Current Justices Stephen Breyer, Samuel Alito, and Anthony Kennedy are the only Justices to have had peacetime military experience.[105] Justices Breyer and Alito have both served in the Army Reserve: Alito as a captain, and Breyer as a corporal. Justice Kennedy served in the National Guard as a private first class.

EDUCATIONAL BACKGROUND

To date, every Supreme Court Justice has been a lawyer. There is, however, no constitutional requirement regarding the educational background of a Justice or the necessity of a law degree. The legal education of many, though not all, Supreme Court Justices reflects the best training available at the time, whether that meant "reading the law" with a prominent attorney or attending an elite law school.

Type of Legal Training

For the first 75 years of the nation, modern legal education as conducted by standard programs administered by law schools did not exist.[106] Some of the most privileged Justices traveled to England for their legal education to study at one of the four Inns of Court, which, from the 14th century to the middle of the 19th century, provided legal training to laypersons and admitted them to the bar.[107] Two of the first five Justices, John Blair and John Rutledge, chose this path and received the bulk of their legal education at the Inn of the Middle Temple in London.

Most Justices, however, trained through an apprenticeship, during which they "read the law." In this apprenticeship, an aspiring attorney would be trained by a practicing attorney. Some lawyers were self-taught. With no standards regarding the qualifications required of a mentor/practicing attorney to take an apprentice and the absence of a common curriculum among mentors, this era has been "dismissively [portrayed] as consisting of shoddy and unscientific training performed haphazardly, either in the law offices of failed attorneys needing to pay the bills or of their successful but overworked counterparts eager to turn their prestige into quick cash."[108]

Of the 111 Justices, 62 (5 5.9%) were educated in whole or in part through reading law. As Figure 8 indicates, the vast majority of Justices appointed between 1789 and 1850 "read the law." During this period, some Justices, such as Chief Justices John Rutledge and John Marshall, both read the law and attended law school.[109] Of the 31 Justices appointed during this time, 27 (87.1%) read the law as their sole means of legal education, 3 (9.7%) attended some law school and read the law, and 1 (3.2%) attended law school.

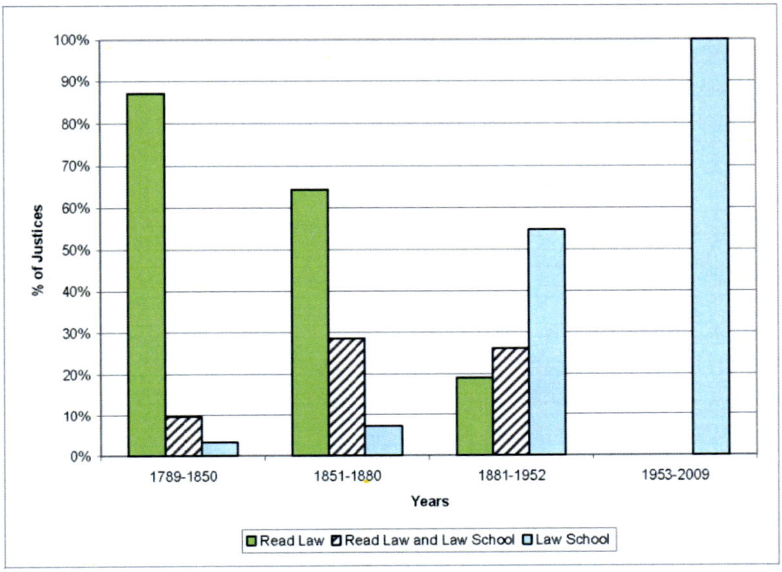

Source: **CRS analysis of data from the Federal Judicial Center's** *Federal Judicial Biographical Database* (www.fjc.gov) and Lee Epstein, Jeffrey A. Segal, Harold J. Spaeth, and Thomas G. Walker, *Supreme Court* Compendium: Data, Decisions, and Developments, 4th ed. (Washington, DC: CQ Press, 2007).

Figure 8. Legal Education of Supreme Court Justices Over Time By Appointment Date and Type of Education, 1789-2009

Of the 111 Justices, 62 (5 5.9%) were educated in whole or in part through reading law. As Figure 8 indicates, the vast majority of Justices appointed **between 1789 and 1850 "read the law." During this period, some Justices,** such as Chief Justices John Rutledge and John Marshall, both read the law and attended law school.[109] Of the 31 Justices appointed during this time, 27 (87.1%) read the law as their sole means of legal education, 3 (9.7%) attended some law school and read the law, and 1 (3.2%) attended law school.

While not the first law school in the United States, the reopening of Harvard Law School in 1829 is generally viewed as the beginning of the modern era in legal education.[110] The movement toward standardized legal education is reflected in the education of Justices appointed between 1851 and 1880. Of the 14 Justices appointed in this period, 64.3% (nine Justices) read the law as their sole method of legal education, as compared with 87.1% (27 of 31 appointed) prior to 1851. Between 1851 and 1880, 28.6% (four Justices) of those appointed both attended law school and read the law, and 7.1% (one Justice) attended law school as their sole means of legal education.

As indicated in Figure 8, between 1881 and 1952, many more Justices attended law school than in the previous two periods. Importantly, the number of Justices who read law as their sole means of legal education or read law in addition to attending law school dropped precipitously. Of the 42 Justices appointed during this period, 23 (54.8%) attended law school and did not read law, 8 (19.0%) read law but did not attend law school, and 11 (26.2%) received both types of training.

The last Justice to be appointed without a formal law degree was Justice James Byrnes, appointed in 1941 by President Franklin D. Roosevelt. Byrnes, who was a U.S. Senator at the time of appointment, had read law between 1896 and 1903; he was self-taught.

All 24 Justices appointed since 1953 were trained at law schools and, unlike many Justices in previous periods, obtained a formal law degree. By this time, the structure of modern legal education was firmly in place and members of the bar, including Supreme Court Justices, were no longer trained through apprenticeship.

Law School Education

Justices since 1909, as **Figure 9** shows, have increasingly received their legal training at Harvard, Yale, or Columbia. Of the 50 Justices appointed in the past 100 years, 46 (92.0%) received part, if not all, of their legal education at a law school. Of these 46 Justices, 22 (47.8%) were trained at Harvard, Columbia, or Yale.

Since 1988, Justices from these three schools have consistently composed **over 50% of the Court's membership**. Each of the nine Justices appointed since the elevation of William Rehnquist to Chief Justice in 1986 has received his or her legal training at Harvard, Yale, or Columbia.[111] The only sitting Justice who did not graduate from Harvard, Yale, or Columbia is John Paul Stevens, who received his law degree from Northwestern University in 1947.

The appointment of Justice Sonia Sotomayor has produced little change in the composition of the Court with respect to legal education. Like Justices Clarence Thomas and Samuel Alito, Judge Sotomayor attended Yale University and replaced David H. Souter, a Harvard alumnus. As a result, the number of Harvard-educated Justices on the Court has been reduced from five to four in the current Court, and the number of Yale-educated Justices has increased from two to three.

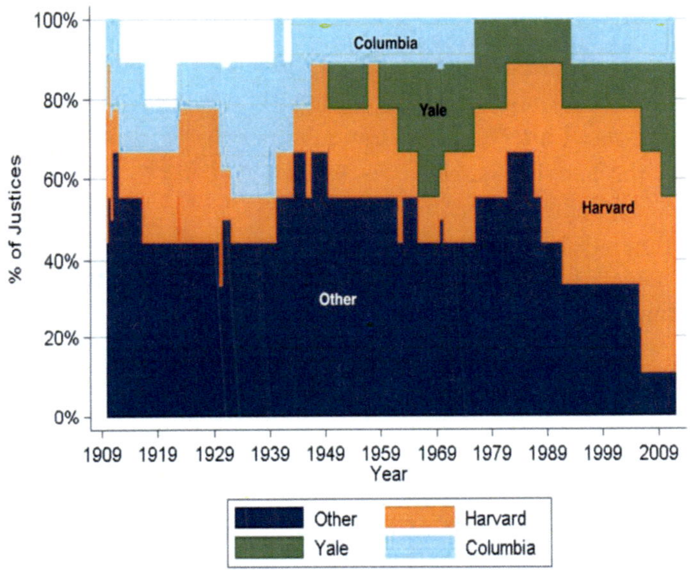

Source: CRS analysis of data from the Federal Judicial Center's *Federal Judicial Biographical Database (*www.fjc.gov) and Lee Epstein, Jeffrey A. Segal, Harold J. Spaeth, and Thomas G. Walker, *Supreme Court Compendium: Data, Decisions, and Developments*, 4th ed. (Washington, DC: CQ Press, 2007).

Notes: The figure displays the percentage of sitting Justices attending Harvard, Yale, or Columbia, All other law schools are represented in the "Other" category. For example, during the third natural court of the Chief Justiceship of Charles Evans Hughes in 1935, Justice Pierce Butler was the only Justice to have not attended a law school. Of the eight Justices who attended law school, three attended Columbia and one each attended Harvard, Virginia, Michigan, Cincinnati, and the University of Pennsylvania. The three attending Columbia (33.3% of sitting Justices) are represented by band at the top of the graph, labeled "Columbia." The one Justice who attended Harvard (11.1% of sitting Justices) is represented by the narrower band, labeled "Harvard." The law school affiliations of the remaining four Justices (44.4% of sitting Justices) is represented by the large band at the bottom of the graph, labeled "Other."

Figure 9. Law Schools Attended by Supreme Court Justices Percentage of Sitting Justices Who Attended Law School, 1909-2009

Conclusion

Since President Obama announced the nomination of Sonia Sotomayor in May 2009, Senators, media commentators, and scholars have engaged in renewed discussion regarding the social, professional, and educational diversity of the Court's membership. Discussion about the importance and appropriate role of a nominee's background is not new. It has been debated widely since the Carter Administration's efforts to diversify the federal judiciary in the late 1970s. Such discussions will likely continue with each future Supreme Court nomination.

Over time, the membership of the Supreme Court has become more diverse in some ways and more homogeneous in others. When the Court was first constituted and throughout most of its history, neither women nor minorities served on the Court. This changed with the appointment of the first African-American Justice, Thurgood Marshall, in 1967, and continued with the appointment of Justice Marshall's replacement, Clarence Thomas, in 1991. The historical makeup of the Court changed yet again with the selection of Justice Sandra Day O'Connor in 1981. She was subsequently joined by Ruth Bader Ginsburg in 1993. The appointment of Sonia Sotomayor has added additional diversity to the Court's membership. Confirmed on August 6, 2009, Sotomayor is the third woman and the first Latina to be appointed to the Court.

The religious affiliations of the Justices have changed over time, as well. For the first 50 years of the Court, all Justices were affiliated with protestant Christian churches. The first Catholic Justice, Chief Justice Roger Brooke Taney, was appointed in 1836. After his appointment, increasing numbers of Roman Catholic Justices have been appointed. Six (66.7%) of the eight Justices on the current Court identify as Roman Catholic, including recently appointed Justice Sonia Sotomayor. The first Jewish Justice, Louis Brandeis, was appointed in 1916. For the next 50 years, at least one Jewish Justice served on the Court until the resignation of Abe Fortas in 1969. Currently, two Jewish Justices, Ruth Bader Ginsburg and Stephen G. Breyer, serve on the Court.

While the Court has become more diverse with respect to race and gender, the career experiences of Justices have become more homogeneous over time. Historically, Justices served in a variety of professions in the public and private sector prior to their elevation. Some have been members of presidential Cabinets, others were governors, members of federal or state legislative bodies, or engaged in private legal practice. During the last 50 years, however, Justices have more and more frequently been elevated from positions on the federal circuit courts of appeals. Of the currently serving Justices, all possess federal circuit court experience. Only one served on a trial court at the state or federal level. Six of the nine current Justices were government attorneys in some capacity. No sitting Justice has served as a federal or state executive or legislator. Notably, only five have prior experience in private practice, as compared with 98.0% (100) of the other 102 Justices elevated to the bench throughout the history of the Court.

The legal educations of the Justices have become more homogeneous, as well. Before the standardization of modern legal education, many Justices pursued their legal education through "reading the law" as an apprentice to a mentoring attorney and supplemented their education through formal legal training at the nation's burgeoning law schools. As legal education became increasingly standardized, an ever-growing number of Justices earned law degrees. Throughout the history of the Court, and especially in the last 20 years, three Ivy League law schools— Harvard, Yale, and Columbia—have been disproportionately represented on the Court. Of the nine sitting Justices, eight attended one of these three schools.

Movement toward greater racial, ethnic, and gender diversity on the Court, as well as patterns of career and education homogenization, reflect both changes in American society and changes in the Senate confirmation process over time. The participation of women and minorities in civic life has led, since the late 1 960s, to greater representation of these groups in the federal judiciary, generally, and the Supreme Court, specifically. For example, Jimmy Carter sought to increase the numbers of women and minorities in the federal courts throughout his presidency, and Ronald Reagan explicitly sought a woman to fill the first Supreme Court vacancy of his Presidency.

Importantly, since the 1950s, the Court has increasingly considered cases with widespread, highly publicized, and controversial social consequences. The Court's often contentious decisions involving issues such as racial segregation, defendants' rights, and personal privacy led to greater scrutiny of Supreme Court nominees by interest groups, media commentators, and the U.S. Senate. Whereas earlier nominees were often confirmed with little Senate scrutiny, extended Senate confirmation hearings have become a routine component of the modern Supreme Court appointment process. Presidents, as a result, have reportedly selected nominees with federal appellate court experience and sterling educational credentials to better predict the nominee's judicial philosophy and insulate the nominee from questions of competency in an increasingly rigorous Senate confirmation process.

End Notes

[1] Letter from David H. Souter, Associate Justice of the United States Supreme Court, to Barack Obama, President of the United States, May 1, 2009, *http://www.supremecourtus. gov/ publicinfo/press/pr_05-01-09.html.*

[2] See U.S. President (Obama), "Remarks on the Nomination of Sonia Sotomayor to be a Supreme Court Justice, May 26, 2009," *Daily Compilation of Presidential Documents*, DCPD-200900402,http://www.gpo.gov/fdsys/pkg/DCPD-200900402/html/DCPD-200900402.htm

[3] For more information about the criteria used by Presidents in the selection of nominees, please see CRS Report RL3 1989, *Supreme Court Appointment Process: Roles of the President, Judiciary Committee, and Senate*.

[4] Some scholars argue, however, that demographic characteristics have little value in explaining judges' decision- making. For an overview of this argument, see Jeffrey Segal and Harold Spaeth, *The Supreme Court and the Attitudinal Model* (Cambridge: Cambridge University Press, 1993), pp. 23 1-234.

[5] The White House, Office of the Press Secretary, "Judge Sonia Sotomayor," , May 26, 2009, *http://www.whitehouse.gov/the_press_office/Background-on-Judge-Sonia-Sotomayor/.*

[6] For a discussion of President Carter's efforts and the opposition he faced, see Sheldon Goldman, "Carter Reforms Judicial Selection," in *Picking Federal Judges: Lower Court Selection from Roosevelt through Reagan* (New Haven, CT: Yale University Press, 1997), pp. 23 6-284. More recently, for a discussion of the perceived pressure on President George W. Bush to appoint a woman to the Court, see, for example, Elizabeth Bumiller, "Pillow-Talk Call for a Woman to fill O'Connor Seat," *The New York Times,* July 18, 2005, p. A13, Late Edition (Final). Additionally, scholars have examined the relationship between race, gender, and judging in the federal courts since the Carter Administration. See, for example, Thomas G. Walker and Deborah J. Barrow, "The Diversification of the Federal Bench: Policy and Process Ramifications," *The Journal of Politics*, vol. 47, no. 2 (June 1985), pp. 596-617; Barbara A. Perry, *A "Representative" Supreme Court? The Impact of Race, Religion, and Gender on Appointments.* (New York: Greenwood Press, 1991); Jennifer A. Segal, "Representative Decision Making on the Federal Bench: Clinton's District Court Appointees," *Political Research Quarterly*, vol. 53, no. 2 (March 2000), pp.138-140. See also Jeffrey Segal and Harold Spaeth, *The Supreme Court and the Attitudinal Model* (Cambridge: Cambridge University Press, 1993), pp. 231-234.

[7] For a discussion of the role of these issues in the Sotomayor nomination, see, for example, Peter Baker, "Court Choice Brings Issue of 'Identity' Back to the Forefront," *New York Times*, May 30, 2009, p. A20, Late Edition (Final).

[8] Some scholars suggest that judges with experience as government attorneys may tend to rule in favor of the government more often than their colleagues without such experience. See, for example, C. Neal Tate and Panu Sittiwong, "Decision Making in the Canadian Supreme Court: Extending the Personal Attributes Model Across Nations," *Journal of Politics*, vol. 51 (Nov. 1989), pp. 911-912; Mark A. Cohen, "Explaining Judicial Behavior, or What's 'Unconstitutional' about the Sentencing Commission?" *Journal of Law, Economics, and Organization*, vol. 7, no. 1 (Spring 1991), pp.1 83-199, 196; and Theodore Eisenberg and Sherri Lynn Johnson, "The Effects of Intent: Do We Know How Legal Standards Work?" *Cornell Law Review*, vol. 76, no. 6 (Sept. 1991), pp.1151-1197, 1190.

[9] In particular, scholars have examined the influence of prior judicial experience on judges' behavior from a multitude of perspectives. For example, some scholars have studied the relationship between prior judicial experience and the predictability of Justices' decision making on the Court. For a discussion of this, see Edward V. Heck and Melinda Gann Hall, "Bloc Voting and the Freshman Justice Revisited," *Journal of Politics,* vol. 43, no. 3 (Aug. 1981), pp.852- 860; David W. Allen, "Voting Blocs and the Freshman Justice on State Supreme Courts," *The Western Political Quarterly*, vol. 44, no. 3 (Sept. 1991), pp. 727-747;

Timothy M. Hagle, "'Freshman Effects' for Supreme Court Justices," *American Journal of Political Science*, vol. 37, no. 4 (Nov. 1993), pp.1 142-1157; John Szmer and Donald R. Songer, "The Effects of Information on the Accuracy of Presidential Assessments of Supreme Court Nominee Preferences," *Political Research Quarterly*, vol. 58, no. 1 (March 2005), pp.15 1-160. Others have examined whether Justices with prior judicial experience author higher-quality opinions. See, for example, Felix Frankfurter, "The Supreme Court in the Mirror of Justices," *University of Pennsylvania Law Review*, vol. 105, no. 6 (April 1957), pp. 78 1-796; William E. Hulbary and Thomas G. Walker, "The Supreme Court Selection Process: Presidential Motivations and Judicial Performance," *The Western Political Quarterly*, vol. 33, no. 2 (June 1980), pp. 185-196; Gregory A. Caldeira, "In the Mirror of the Justices: Sources of Greatness on the Supreme Court," *Political Behavior*, vol. 10, no. 3 (Autumn 1988), pp. 247-266; Montgomery N. Kosma, "Measuring the Influence of Supreme Court Justices," *The Journal of Legal Studies*, vol. 27, no. 2 (June 1998), pp. 333-372. For an examination of United States Courts of Appeals judges, see William M. Landes, Lawrence Lessig, and Michael E. Solimine, "Judicial influence: A Citation Analysis of Federal Courts of Appeals Judges," *The Journal of Legal Studies*, vol. 27, no. 2 (June 1998), pp. 27 1-332.

[10] Some scholars suggest that Justices with prior military experience may have a distinct view of the role of the executive. For an example, see Gregory C. Sisk, Michael Heise, and Andrew P. Morris, "Charting the Influence on the Judicial Mind: An Empirical Study of Judicial Reasoning," *New York University Law Review*, vol. 73, no. 5 (November 1998), pp. 1439.

[11] In particular, it has been argued that while law schools generally share the common purpose of "nourish[ing] and transmit[ting] the Anglo-American legal tradition" through a well-documented socialization process, each law school may impart its own institutional perspective. This may be especially true for Ivy League institutions, such as Harvard, Yale, and Columbia, "which ... have changed slowly over time [and] may themselves have fostered a particular culture of legal education." See Daniel J. Meador, "Lawyers and Legal Education in the South: A Proposed Study," *Tennessee Law Review*, vol. 30 (Summer 1963), p. 540; Lani Guiner, Michelle Fine, and Jane Balin, "Becoming Gentlemen: Women's Experiences at One Ivy League Law School," *University of Pennsylvania Law Review*, vol. 143, no. 1 (Nov. 1994), pp. 3.

[12] Lee Epstein, Jack Knight, and Andrew D. Martin, "The Norm of Prior Judicial Experience and Its Consequences for Career Diversity on the U.S. Supreme Court," *California Law Review*, vol. 91, no. 4 (July 2003), p. 944.

[13] Ibid., p. 944.

[14] For a discussion of these themes, see generally Lee Epstein and Thomas G. Walker, *Constitutional Law for a Changing America: Rights, Liberties, and Justice*, Sixth Edition (Washington, DC: CQ Press, 2006); and Lee Epstein and Thomas G. Walker, *Constitutional Law for a Changing America: Institutional Powers and Constraints*, Sixth Edition (Washington, DC: CQ Press, 2006).

[15] For an in-depth discussion of the criteria used by Presidents to select Supreme Court nominees in the first 61 years of the Court's history, see Henry J. Abraham, "Chapter Five: The First Forty Years: From George Washington to John Quincy Adams, 1789-1829" and "Chapter Six: The Next Forty Years: From Andrew Jackson to Andrew Johnson, 1829-1869," *Justices and Presidents: A Political History of Appointments to the Supreme Court*, Third Edition (New York: Oxford University Press, 1992), pp. 7 1-125.

[16] Abraham, *Justices and Presidents*, p. 110.

[17] Ibid., pp. 110-136.

[18] Ibid., pp. 241.

[19] Ibid., pp. 241.

[20] Ibid., pp. 254.

[21] 347 U.S. 483 (1954). This decision effectively overruled the separate-but-equal doctrine, mandating the desegregation of public schools with "all deliberate speed." For a discussion

of desegregation cases in a broader context, see Epstein and Walker, *Constitutional Law for a Changing America: Rights, Liberties, and Justice*, pp. 661- 696.

[22] 374 U.S. 203 (1963). This decision found that mandatory religious activities in public schools, such as the recitation of the Lord's Prayer and the reading of Bible verses, is a violation of both the Free Exercise Clause and the Establishment Clause of the First Amendment, even if the school allows a student to be exempted from such activities with parental permission. For a discussion of Supreme Court cases concerning prayer in school, see Epstein and Walker, *Constitutional Law for a Changing America: Rights, Liberties, and Justice*, pp. 196–213.

[23] 77 U.S. 533 (1964). This decision promulgated the "one man, one vote" principle, which required states to apportion state and federal legislative districts based on population. For a discussion of landmark Supreme Court cases concerning voting rights, see Epstein and Walker, *Constitutional Law for a Changing America: Rights, Liberties, and Justice*, pp. 809-823.

[24] Abraham, *Justices and Presidents*, p. 254.

[25] David A. Yalof, *The Pursuit of Justices: Presidential Politics and the Selection of Supreme Court Nominees* (Chicago: The University of Chicago Press, 1999), p. 70.

[26] Both of Kennedy's appointees and Johnson's first nomination of Abe Fortas to Associate Justice encountered very little opposition, with their confirmation hearings before the Senate Judiciary Committee lasting no more than two days. For more information regarding the Supreme Court appointment process generally and the length of nominations specifically, see CRS Report RL3 1989, *Supreme Court Appointment Process: Roles of the President, Judiciary Committee, and Senate*; and CRS Report RL3 3225, *Supreme Court Nominations, 1789 - 2009: Actions by the Senate, the Judiciary Committee, and the President*, respectively.

[27] Yalof, *The Pursuit of Justices*, p.130.

[28] Ibid., p.131.

[29] Ibid., p.121.

[30] See, for example, Yalof's discussion of Presidents Richard Nixon's and Ronald Reagan's searches in chapters five and six of *The Pursuit of Justice*, pp. 97-167.

[31] One important factor, geography, is not discussed in this report. For an account of the importance of geography in the selection process, see generally Abraham, *Justices and Presidents*. For a more focused and systematic study of geographical representation on the Court, see William J. Daniels, "The Geographic Factor in Appointments to the United States Supreme Court: 1789-1976," *The Western Political Quarterly*, vol. 31, no. 2 (June 1978), pp. 226-23 7.

[32] See CRS Report RL3 3225, *Supreme Court Nominations, 1789 - 2009: Actions by the Senate, the Judiciary Committee, and the President*, p. 35.

[33] Of the 106 Supreme Court nominations reported out from the Senate Judiciary Committee to the full Senate, only 4 have been reported without recommendation, one of which was the nomination of Clarence Thomas. Ibid., pp. 9, 38.

[34] Scholars debate whether Justice Benjamin Cardozo, whose family roots are believed to trace back to Portugal, was the first Hispanic to serve on the Court. In modern usage, the terms "Hispanic" and "Latino" are terms of self- identification, used inconsistently by individuals who were born or whose ancestors were born in over 20 Spanish-speaking countries. At the time of Cardozo's appointment in the 1930s, such terms were not used in the census. For example, the only identifier used to count the Hispanic population was that of "Mexican." When asked how Justice Cardozo would self-identify, a biographer of the Justice answered, "I think he would have identified as a Sephardic Jew whose ancestors came from the Iberian Peninsula." According to a report by the Pew Hispanic Center, Justice Cardozo would not qualify as Hispanic by current census standards, which do not identify individuals of Portuguese descent as Hispanic. As a result, Justice Sotomayor is the first Hispanic or Latina Justice to serve on the Supreme Court, at least by census standards. For an overview

of this issue, see Neil A. Lewis, "Was Hispanic on Court in the '30s?" *New York Times*, May 27, 2009, p. A16, Late Edition (Final); Jeffrey Passel and Paul Taylor, *Who's Hispanic*, Pew Hispanic Center, Washington, DC, May 29, 2009, *http://pew hispanic.org/ files/reports/111.pdf.*

[35] Sonia Sotomayor, "A Latina Judge's Voice," *Berkeley La Raza Law Journal,* vol. 13, no. 1 (Spring 2002), p. 88.

[36] Ibid.

[37] Abraham, *Justices and Presidents,* p. 339.

[38] Mark Silverstein, *Judicious Choices: The New Politics of Supreme Court Confirmations* (New York: W.W. Norton and Company, 1994), p. 167. Thurgood Marshall served as assistant special counsel for the NAACP and, in that role, was one of the architects of the NAACP's legal strategy that eventually led to the landmark 1954 Supreme Court decision *Brown v. Topeka Board of Education* (347 U.S. 483), in which the Supreme Court which found that racial segregation based on the separate-but-equal doctrine was a violation of the Equal Protection Clause of the Fourteenth Amendment. From 1940 through 1961, Marshall argued successfully before the Court in 29 separate cases. Marshall was appointed to the Supreme Court in 1967 by President Lyndon Johnson. Ruth Bader Ginsburg, like Marshall, was the architect of the ACLU's legal strategy with respect to women's rights. Notably, in 1971, Ginsburg successfully argued *Reed v. Reed* (404 U.S. 71) before the Supreme Court, in which the Court found that an Idaho statute that, in determining the executor of an estate of a minor who has died intestate, gave preference to men over women was a violation of the Equal Protection Clause of the Fourteenth Amendment. Ginsburg successfully argued five gender discrimination cases before the Supreme Court.

[39] After 24 years of service on the Supreme Court, Justice O'Connor announced her retirement from the Court on July 1, 2005, effective upon the start of the next October term or the appointment of her successor. See Letter from Sandra Day O'Connor, Associate Justice of the Supreme Court of the United States, to George W. Bush, President of the United States, July 1, 2005, http://www.supremecourtus.gov/publicinfo/press/oconnor070105.pdf.

[40] Jan Crawford Greenburg, "Bush advisers alter Court focus; Aides said to push conservative males to replace O'Connor," *Chicago Tribune*, July 19, 2005, p. C8; Steven Thommas and Stephen Henderson, "Bush Picks Roberts for Chief Justice; Speculation on Who Will Fill Other Seat," *Monterey County Herald*, Sept. 6, 2005, Section Z (Nation); Christina L. Boyd and Lee Epstein, "Female Justices vital," *The Virginian-Pilot*, May 5, 2009, p. B7.

[41] Laura Mecoy, "O'Connor's advice: Pick a woman," *Sacramento Bee*, Oct. 28, 2005, p. A22, Final Edition.

[42] Miers requested that her nomination be withdrawn after Senators requested privileged White House documents from Miers's tenure as White House counsel to evaluate her record. For a more comprehensive account of the nomination of Harriet Miers to the Supreme Court, see Jeffrey Toobin, "Chapter 22: I Know Her Heart," in *The Nine: Inside the Secret World of the Supreme Court* (New York: Doubleday, 2007), pp. 284-297. See also CRS Report RL33 118, *Speed of Presidential and Senate Actions on Supreme Court Nominations, 1900-2009.*

[43] The Episcopal Church, a protestant church deriving from the Church of England, was established in the American colonies with the Jamestown colony in 1607. After the Revolutionary War, all English public support for the church ceased. Though relatively impoverished, by this time the church had spread widely through the colonies, especially in the southern and middle colonies. See Theodore Dwight Woolsey et al., *The First Century of the Republic: A View of American Progress* (New York: Harper and Brothers, 1876), p. 480; Episcopal Church of the United States, "Newsline: Anglican and Episcopal Church History," Accessed July 14, 2009, http://www.episcopalchurch.org/ newsline_22035_ ENG_HTM.htm.

[44] These Justices were Joseph McKenna of California and Edward D. White of Louisiana. McKenna was appointed by President William McKinley in 1898; White was appointed by President Grover Cleveland in 1894.

[45] Abraham, *Justices and Presidents,* pp. 182-185. Additionally, Justice Brandeis encountered some hostility on the Court itself. Justice James McReynolds, appointed by President Wilson in 1914, was reported to be anti-Semitic and "snubbed" Brandeis for that reason. See also David Burner, *The Justices of the Supreme Court, 1789-1969: Their Lives and Major Opinions*, ed. Leon Friedman and Fred L. Israel, vol. 3 (New York: Chelsea House Publishers, 1969), p. 2023.

[46] Brandeis's confirmation hearings were also the first ever public hearings held by the Judiciary Committee to examine the nomination of an individual to the Supreme Court. Only one other nominee, George Williams, nominated to the position of Chief Justice by President Ulysses S. Grant in 1873, had ever received a hearing. Unlike Brandeis's hearing, Williams's confirmation hearing was closed to the public. See CRS Report RL3 3225, *Supreme Court Nominations, 1789 - 2009: Actions by the Senate, the Judiciary Committee, and the President.*

[47] Cardozo was appointed by President Herbert Hoover shortly before the end of his first and final term in 1932. Frankfurter was appointed by President Franklin Roosevelt, a close friend, after Cardozo's death in 1939.

[48] Abraham, *Justices and Presidents*, p. 206.

[49] Ibid., p. 222.

[50] Ibid. Abraham notes that Frankfurter's appearance before the committee was the first since the nomination of Harlan Fiske Stone to the position of Associate Justice in 1925.

[51] CRS Report RL3 3225, *Supreme Court Nominations, 1789 - 2009: Actions by the Senate, the Judiciary Committee, and the President.*

[52] The average length of a public hearing, for all public hearings held between 1916 and the present, is 3.97 days. In the last 20 years, the average length of public hearings has increased by almost a full day to 4.91 days.

[53] Byron "Whizzer" White, appointed by President John F. Kennedy in 1962, was a Heisman Trophy winning football player at the University of Colorado and played professional football for the Pittsburgh Pirates (now Steelers). During his one season in professional football, he was the highest-paid player of his day. See, for more information, Yalof, *The Pursuit of Justices*, pp. 73-76, and Cushman, "Byron R. White" in *The Supreme Court Justices: Illustrated Biographies, 1789-1993*, pp. 461-465.

[54] The first of these Justices to be appointed was Samuel Chase of Maryland, who was appointed by George Washington in 1796. The second was Chase's replacement, Gabriel Duvall (also of Maryland), who was appointed by James Madison in 1811.

[55] U.S. attorneys prosecute criminal offenses against the United States, prosecute or defend for the government all suits or proceedings in which the United States is concerned, and collect debts owed the federal government which are administratively uncollectible. U.S. attorneys are appointed to four-year terms and serve at the pleasure of the President. There are, in total, 93 U.S. attorneys: one for each federal judicial district, with the exception of the District of Guam and the District of the Northern Mariana Islands, which share a U.S. attorney. For more information on the responsibilities of U.S. attorneys, see 28 U.S.C. 547.

[56] Associate Justices James Iredell and Alfred Moore both served as the attorney general of North Carolina. Iredell served in that positions from 1779 through 1781, and Moore served from 1782 through 1791. Associate Justice William Paterson served as the attorney general of New Jersey from 1776 through 1783. Justice John Rutledge, who served as both an Associate Justice and, for a brief period of time, Chief Justice, served as the Attorney General Pro Tem from 1764 through 1765, before the signing of the Declaration of Independence. Chief Justice Roger Brooke Taney served as the attorney general of Maryland from 1827 through 1831.

[57] Justices Henry Baldwin, John Catron, and Robert Trimble served as district attorneys in Pennsylvania, Tennessee, and Kentucky, respectively. Additionally, Chief Justice Oliver Ellsworth served as a state attorney in Hartford County, Connecticut from 1777 through 1785.

[58] Justice Nathan Clifford served as both the attorney general for the state of Maine (1834-1838) and the U.S. Attorney General (1846-1848); Justice John Marshall Harlan served as the attorney general for the state of Kentucky (1863- 1867).

[59]Justice Noah Swayne served as both the prosecuting attorney for Coshocton County, Ohio (1826-1829), and U.S. attorney for the district of Ohio (1830-1841).

[60] This report does not examine whether those appointed to the Chief Justiceship possessed experience as an Associate Justice. Additionally, Chief Justices were occasionally elevated from the ranks of Associate Justices or had prior experience as an Associate Justice, as was the case with Chief Justices John Rutledge, Edward White, Charles Evans Hughes, Harlan Fiske Stone, and William Rehnquist. John Rutledge served as an Associate Justice from 1789 through 1791, resigning to serve as the Chief Justice of the South Carolina Court of Common Pleas. In 1795, George Washington appointed Rutledge to be Chief Justice via a recess appointment after the resignation of John Jay. Rutledge was not confirmed by the Senate and was forced to resign his position that same year. Charles Evans Hughes served as an Associate Justice from 1910 through 1916, when he resigned to run as the Republican candidate for President. After losing to Woodrow Wilson, Hughes went into private practice and later served as U.S. Secretary of State before being appointed to the position of Chief Justice in 1930. Chief Justices White, Stone, and Rehnquist were all elevated directly from the position of Associate Justice.

[61] The Judiciary Act of 1789 required that two Supreme Court Justices sit with a district court judge to constitute the circuit court. This requirement was changed in 1793 to allow one Justice and a district court judge to constitute a circuit court. Federal Judicial Center, "Courts of the Federal Judiciary: U.S. Circuit Courts and the Federal Judiciary," http://www.fjc.gov/public/home.nsf/hisc.

[62] See Federal Judicial Center, "Courts of the Federal Judiciary: U.S. Circuit Courts and the Federal Judiciary."

[63] The location of the nation's capital has changed several times, and the meeting place of the Supreme Court has changed with it. The first meeting of the Court occurred on February 2, 1790, in the Merchants Exchange Building in New York City. Later that year, the Court moved with the federal government to Philadelphia, where the Court met first in Independence Hall and later in City Hall. In 1800, the Court, along with the executive and legislative branches, moved permanently to the District of Columbia. See U.S. Supreme Court, "The Court Building," http://www.supremecourtus.gov/about/courtbuilding.pdf.

[64] Wilson was one of the original six justices of the Supreme Court, appointed by George Washington in 1789. See Jeffrey A. Segal, Harold J. Spaeth, and Sara C. Benesh, *The Supreme Court in the American Legal System* (Cambridge: Cambridge University Press, 2005), p. 216.

[65] From 1891 through 1912, the circuit courts retained their original jurisdiction and served as trial courts for some types of federal cases. See Federal Judicial Center, "Courts of the Federal Judiciary: U.S. Circuit Courts and the Federal Judiciary," *http://www.fjc.gov/public/home.nsf/hisc.*

[66] The percentage of sitting Justices with state court experience dropped to 44.4% between 1842 and 1845.

[67] Justice Stephen Field was elevated from the California supreme court, on which he had served as Chief Justice, to the U.S. Supreme Court by Abraham Lincoln in 1863.

[68] Abraham, *Justices and Presidents*, pp. 110, 114-115, 117.

[69] Ibid., p. 110.

[70] Ibid., p. 117.

[71] Ibid., pp. 137-139.

[72] Ibid., p. 140. In particular, Abraham noted that President Cleveland's criteria were "easy to behold."

[73] Ibid., p. 148.

[74] Abraham, *Justices and Presidents*, p. 157.

75 Ibid., p. 167.

76 Ibid., pp. 176-177.

77 Franklin D. Roosevelt's one appointee with federal judicial experience was Wiley B. Rutledge, who had served on the D.C. Circuit Court of Appeals.

78 Truman's sole Associate Justice appointee with judicial experience was Sherman Minton, who had served on the Seventh Circuit Court of Appeals.

79 During this period, President Herbert Hoover's appointees were the exception to this trend. Hoover reportedly sought candidates with prior judicial experience, and two of his three appointees had served as judges at the state or federal level. Charles Evans Hughes, Hoover's choice for Chief Justice, had previously served as an Associate Justice, and Benjamin Cardozo, one of Hoover's selections for Associate Justice, was a widely regarded jurist on the supreme court of New York. Hoover's only selection without judicial experience, Justice Owen Roberts, was selected after John J. Parker, a sitting judge on the U.S. Court of Appeals for the Fourth Circuit, was rejected by the Senate. See Abraham, *Justices and Presidents*, pp. 198-207.

80 Abraham, *Justices and Presidents*, p. 254.

81 For a discussion of the use of patronage politics in Kennedy's and Johnson's selections of Supreme Court nominees, see Yalof, "Chapter Four: Kennedy and Johnson Restore the Politics of Patronage," *The Pursuit of Justices*, pp. 70-96.

82 Both of Kennedy's appointees and Johnson's first nomination of Abe Fortas to Associate Justice encountered very little opposition, with their confirmation hearings before the Senate Judiciary Committee lasting no more than two days. For more information regarding the Supreme Court appointment process generally and the length of nominations specifically, see CRS Report RL3 1989, *Supreme Court Appointment Process: Roles of the President, Judiciary Committee, and Senate*; and CRS Report RL3 3225, *Supreme Court Nominations, 1789 - 2009: Actions by the Senate, the Judiciary Committee, and the President*, respectively.

83 Yalof, *The Pursuit of Justices*, p.130.

84 Other problems, such as Justice Fortas's alleged financial improprieties and President Johnson's "lame duck" status complicated an already hostile Senate reception to the nomination. See Yalof, "Chapter Four: Kennedy and Johnson Restore the Politics of Patronage," *The Pursuit of Justices*, pp. 70-96.

85 Yalof, *Pursuit of Justices*, p. 70.

86 Ibid., p. 121.

87 Ibid., p. 170.

88 The two Justices with both federal district and circuit court experience are Justice Charles Whittaker, appointed in 1957 by President Dwight D. Eisenhower, and Sonia Sotomayor, appointed in 2009 by President Barack Obama.

89 Justice David H. Souter, appointed by President George H.W. Bush in 1990, served on both the New Hampshire Supreme Court and the U.S. Court of Appeals for the First Circuit.

90 Justices Ruth Bader Ginsburg, Antonin Scalia, Clarence Thomas, and Chief Justice John Roberts served on the U.S. Court of Appeals for the D.C. Circuit; Justice Stephen Breyer on the First Circuit; Justice Sonia Sotomayor on the Second Circuit; Justice Samuel Alito on the Third Circuit; Justice John Paul Stevens on the Seventh Circuit; and Justice Anthony Kennedy on the Ninth Circuit.

91 Sonia Sotomayor served on two federal courts before her appointment to the Supreme Court: (1) the District Court for the Southern District of New York for 6.2 years and (2) the U.S. Court of Appeals for the Second Circuit for 10.8 years. On the day of her confirmation, her combined federal service totaled 17.0 years.

92 See U.S. President (Obama), "Remarks on the Nomination of Sonia Sotomayor to be a Supreme Court Associate Justice, May 26, 2009," *Daily Compilation of Presidential Documents*, DCPD-200900402, at *http://www.gpo*.gov/ fdsys/pkg/DCPD-200900402/ html /DCPD-200900402.htm

93 Abraham, *Justices and Presidents*, pp. 72, 77-78.
94 Abraham, *Justices and Presidents*, p. 80.
95 Ibid., p. 91.
96 Ibid., p. 96.
97 Justices who formerly served as presidential appointees have served as Cabinet members, ambassadors, solicitors general, and department heads within agencies, to name a few. For example, Justice William O. Douglas, appointed by President Franklin D. Roosevelt in 1939, had previously served as both a member and chairman of the Securities and Exchange Commission.
98 "From the Washington Administration to the present, there have been eleven separate formal declarations of war against foreign nations enacted by Congress and the President, encompassing five declared wars" These wars are the War of 1812 (declared in 1812), the Mexican-American War (1846), the Spanish-American War (1898), World War I (1917), and World War II (1941, 1942). The United States participated in several "extended military engagements that might be considered undeclared wars," including the Korean War, the Vietnam War, the Persian Gulf War of 1991. "In addition, Congress has adopted a number of authorizations for the use of military force, the most recent being the joint resolution enacted on October 16, 2002, authorizing the use of military force against Iraq." See CRS Report RL3 1133, Declarations of War and Authorizations for the Use of Military Force: Historical Background and Legal Implications, p.1; CRS Report RL32 170, *Instances of Use of United States Armed Forces Abroad, 1798-2008*, Summary.
99 Additionally, one Justice, William Paterson (appointed by George Washington in 1793), served as a minuteman.
100 Justices James M. Wayne and John Catron, both appointed by Justice Andrew Jackson, were the only Justices in this period with military experience to have served in a war other than the Revolutionary War.
101 John Marshall Harlan I and William B. Woods were appointed by Rutherford B. Hayes in 1877 and 1880, respectively.
102 The first, Lucius C.Q. Lamar, had served as a colonel in the Confederate Army and was appointed to the Court by President Grover Cleveland in 1888. The second, Edward Douglass White, who served as a lieutenant, was appointed by Cleveland in 1894. White was later elevated to the position of Chief Justice in 1910 by President William Howard Taft.
103 One of these veterans, Frank Murphy, appointed by Franklin Delano Roosevelt in 1940, also participated in army training as a lieutenant during a Court recess in 1942 during the Second World War. For more information, see Sidney Fine, "Frank Murphy," in *The Supreme Court Justices: Illustrated Biographies, 1789-1993*, ed. Clare Cushman (Washington, DC: Congressional Quarterly, 1993), pp. 396-400.
104 The Army Air Force was the immediate precursor to the modern Air Force. The Army Air Force came into being in 1941, assuming control over the Army Air Corps, which had been in existence since 1926, and the Air Force Combat Command. At this time, the Army Air Force was still a combatant arm of the U.S. Army. See Air Force Historical Research Agency, "Fact Sheet: The Birth of the United States Air Force," http://www.afhra.af.mil/factsheets/factsheet.asp?id=10944/.
105 Justice Alito joined the Army Reserve Officer's Training Corps (ROTC) while a student at Princeton University in the late 1960s. While commissioned as a Second Lieutenant after graduation in 1972, Alito deferred until his graduation from law school in 1975. While Alito's military service technically overlapped with the Vietnam War for several months, he did not begin military service until two years after the termination of the conflict. For an account of Alito's decision to join the military, see "Alito Joined ROTC While at Princeton," *The Washington Post*, November 3, 2005, Final Edition, p. A4.
106 William D. Bader and Roy M. Mersky, *The First One Hundred and Eight Justices* (Buffalo, NY: William S. Hein & Co., 2004), p. 10.

[107] During the 17th and 18th century, many colonists came to study at the inns, and this practice continued until the War of 1812. Today, these four Inns of Court have "the exclusive right to Call men and women to the Bar, i.e. to admit those who have fulfilled the necessary qualifications to the degree of Barrister-at-Law, which entitles them, after a period of pupilage (vocational training) either to practice as independent advocates in the Courts of England and Wales or to take employment in government or local government service, industry, commerce or finance." See The Honourable Society of the Middle Temple, *Middle Temple,* "The Inn," http://www.middletemple.org.uk/.

[108] Andrew M. Siegel, "'To Learn and Make Respectable Hereafter:' The Litchfield Law School in Cultural Context," *New York University Law Review*, vol. 73, no. 6 (Dec. 1998), p. 1979.

[109] Justice John Rutledge attended the Inns of Middle Temple; Justice John Marshall attended William and Mary.

[110] Siegel, "To Learn and Make Respectable Hereafter," p. 1978. While first founded in 1817, Harvard failed to allocate sufficient resources to its law school and struggled with declining enrollment and the long absences of the school's one professor. By 1827, the struggling law school had just one teacher and one student. Legal education at Harvard was reinvigorated by alumnus Nathan Dane, who recruited Supreme Court Justice Joseph Story to serve as the first Dane Professor at Harvard. See also Harvard Law School, "About HLS: Our History," *Harvard Law School Website*, http://www.law.harvard.edu/about/history.html.

[111] Though Justice Ruth Bader Ginsburg (appointed by President Clinton in 1993) received the bulk of her legal education at Harvard, she graduated from Columbia.

INDEX

D

N

O

P

Q

R

S

T

U

V

W